Timeless Seeds of Advice
Part 2

*

A Deeper Reflection

B. B. Abdulla

2023

Dedication

All praise and gratitude are due to Allah ﷻ. May Allah's peace and blessings be on Muhammad ﷺ, his family and his companions. In the name of Allah, The extremely loving and caring, The always loving and caring.

This book is dedicated to those who love Allah ﷻ and His Messenger Muhammad ﷺ, and who seek knowledge to develop themselves for the day they will stand in front of Allah ﷻ. The previous *Timeless Seeds of Advice* book aimed to revive the heart by the permission of Allah ﷻ and bring comfort to one's chest through countless gems. This book aims to move a step further than that by exploring a number of essential topics and delving into their roots to make believers firm in their faith and resolve, like firm trees in a continually moving river. This river today is the changing trends, ideas, and the people around us—the many environmental influences that sway hearts left and right.

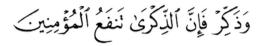

"And go on reminding [people], it is good for those who believe to be reminded." [The Quran, 51:55]

Preface

This book aims to explore and delve deeper into the roots of the sayings discussed in the previous book, *Timeless Seeds of Advice*. The aim of this book is to lend the seeker deeper knowledge of a number of important Quranic verses, supplemented by hadiths of our beloved Messenger Muhammad ﷺ and the insights of the great scholars, consoling their souls with the knowledge that the mercy, love and care of Allah ﷻ are ever near.

The book is divided into sections with numbered titles, following the previous book's format, aimed to be read daily.

The Quran is a book that sheds light on everything we do and encounter in our lives. We cannot see the Quran in the light of something else, but we can see everything in the light of the Quran. It is a lens and a light which allows the believer to see what others will never see. It allows the believer to perceive, think, understand and see differently, making them the true servant of Allah ﷻ.

The root of success in this world and the next is the Quran and its guidance. Shaykh al-Islām Ibn Taymiyyah رحمه الله said: "Remembrance of Allah ﷻ for the heart is like water for fish; and what will be the state of a fish when it is separated from water?"

The content of this book has given me strength and kept me going when the world seemed to close in; when there seemed to be no way out; when I did not know what to do. It has increased me in conviction and strength of heart in facing the countless storms we face in our daily lives.

Anyone who believes in God and the Last Day should heed this: God will find a way out for those who are mindful of Him, and will provide

I

for them from an unexpected source; God will be enough for those who put their trust in Him. God achieves His purpose; God has set a due measure for everything. [From the Quran, 65:2 – 65:3]

Therefore, we start by saying:

$$وَقُل رَّبِّ زِدْنِي عِلْمًا$$

"And say, 'Lord, increase me in knowledge!'" [The Quran, 20:114]

— A servant in need of Allah's mercy

In *sujūd* (prostration), I found my home

This book is composed of three journeys:

The first and the main journey: warning and admonishment as a wakeup call. A revival of the faith in the heart.

The second journey: softening and reviving the heart by removing impurities by way of demonstrating the unlimited mercy of Allah ﷻ.

Lastly: the time to journey back to Allah ﷻ is long overdue, has the time not come to break the locks on your heart? Now that you have received warnings to make your heart tremble, and have seen the unlimited mercy of Allah ﷻ, has the time not come to return back to Allah ﷻ? The journey to Allah ﷻ cannot happen without your most important vehicle: your heart.

Journey 1

Reminders of where you are headed and what you need to take with you as provision and protection

Knowledge to the heart is like water to fish. Arming yourself with knowledge will allow you to grow, purify yourself, and mend your shortcomings. Knowledge will serve as a wake-up call in realizing what is at stake and what needs to be done. Investing your time in seeking it will allow you to rise higher and gain closeness to Allah ﷻ, which is the ultimate peace and comfort of the heart and the soul. This journey will counsel you for the next chapter of your life, the Hereafter (*al-ākhirah*).

Ibn al-Qayyim رَحِمَهُ الله said "Allah ﷻ—free is He from imperfection—has made knowledge for the hearts similar to how He has made rain for the earth; just as there is no life for the earth except with rain, there is no life for the heart except with knowledge."

This page intentionally left blank.

I

You will die, and the final inheritance is to Allah ﷻ. We all have houses in Paradise (Jannah) built for us. Our primary, default destination is salvation, but it is only we who refuse to go thinking it is not worth the effort, losing the inheritance in heaven made for us by our loving Master. Paradise was never out of reach—it has always been in close.

The Prophet ﷺ said: "Everyone from my *ummah* (followers) will enter Paradise except those who refuse." They said, "O Messenger of Allah, who will refuse?" The Prophet ﷺ said, "Whoever obeys me enters Paradise, and whoever disobeys me has refused (to enter it)."[1]

Whenever we spend from our worldly life for the sake of Allah ﷻ, then it is a deposit in our account in the Hereafter. But we make ourselves miserable for the promise of a false future, the belief that our happiness will be in this. The known fact is that the life of this world without Allah ﷻ cannot bring peace or calm; true, long-lasting calm and peace of mind come from the worship of Allah ﷻ.

When you give to Allah ﷻ, Allah ﷻ will give to you. Allah ﷻ is aware of what you do, and He is fully knowledgeable about what you do. He has provided us with every ingredient for living a peaceful life. It must mean we are not doing something right when we do not have such a life.

Ibn al-Jawzī رحمه الله said, "By Allah ﷻ, if you sold one moment of solitary worship of Allah ﷻ for the entire lifespan of Nūḥ ﷵ along with the wealth of Qārūn, you would have lost in the bargain. No, in

---

[1] *Ṣaḥīḥ al-Bukhārī*, no. 7280.

reality, even if you got everything in the heavens in return for that moment, it would not be a profitable sale. And those who have experienced this can attest to its truth."[1]

---

[1] Ibn al-Jawzī, *Seeds of Admonishment and Reform*, p. 93.

2

When you always choose Allah ﷻ, you will get the reward of the Hereafter. The reward of this life may come, or not come, but the Hereafter is guaranteed. When you demonstrate to Allah ﷻ that you want to do good, Allah ﷻ will open different doors for you to do good.

When he was imprisoned, Prophet Yūsuf ﷵ was not seeking relief. Rather, he was seeking to serve Allah ﷻ. And when someone seeks to serve Allah ﷻ, He will make the world serve them like He did for Yūsuf ﷵ; and He will bend the rays of the sun for them like He did for the Companions of the Cave.

> The king said, "Bring him to me: I will have him serve me personally," and then, once he had spoken with him, "From now on you will have our trust and favor." [The Quran, 12:54]

Then the world was made to serve Yūsuf ﷵ.

> In this way We settled Yūsuf in that land to live wherever he wished: We grant Our mercy to whoever We will and do not fail to reward those who do good. [The Quran, 12:56]

And we are reminded yet again the way Allah ﷻ does things.

> The reward of the Hereafter is best for those who believe and are mindful of God. [The Quran, 12:57]

He will bend the rays of the sun for those who seek to serve Him like He did for the Companions of the Cave when they sought refuge with Allah ﷻ from the world:

You could have seen the [light of the] sun as it rose, moving away to the right of their cave, and when it set, moving away to the left of them, while they lay in the wide space inside the cave. This is one of God's signs: those people God guides are rightly guided, but you will find no protector to lead to the right path those He leaves to stray. [The Quran, 18:17]

3

"You'll feel empty for as long as you fill your heart with love of this world. Cultivate love for the Hereafter; it'll fill your heart!"[1]

"I take refuge with Allah ﷻ, and no one else, from *shayṭān* harming me in my religion or diverting me away from a duty that Allah ﷻ has imposed upon me."[2] It is an implicit acknowledgement of the power of Allah ﷻ and one's own weakness and inability to combat the unseen enemy, *shayṭān*. If a person is overcome by a physical enemy, he will be rewarded [for his hardship]; if he is overcome by the unseen enemy, he will be put to severe trial. The servant cannot see *shayṭān* but *shayṭān* can see him, so he in turn takes refuge with One can see *shayṭān* and whom *shayṭān* cannot see.[3]

Ibn al-Qayyim رَحِمَهُ اللهُ said, "It is necessary to know that performing sins is detrimental and harmful to the servant. The harm that sins cause to the heart is comparable to the differing levels of harm that various types of poison cause to the body. Indeed, is there a single evil that occurs in the world or will occur in the Hereafter except that its cause is sin? What caused our parents to be ejected from Paradise, the land of delight, felicity, and joy, to the land of pain, misery, and affliction? What caused Iblīs [Satan] to be ejected from enjoying the company of the angels to being debased and cursed? What caused his outward and inward form to be disfigured such that he took on the vilest of features and his inner features even worse? What caused him to become distant [from Allah ﷻ] after being close; from being a recipient of His mercy to being a recipient of His curse; from being

---

[1] Mufti Menk, Motivational Moments Part II.
[2] Al-Ṭabarī, vol. 1, pg. 76.
[3] Ibn Kathīr, vol. 1, pg. 34.

beautiful to being ugly; from being in Paradise to being condemned to the blazing Fire; from being a believer to being a disbeliever; from being the friend of Allah ﷻ to being His greatest enemy; from being a person devoted to the glorification of his Lord to being a person of *kufr*, *shirk*, lies and shameful deeds; from wearing the raiment of faith to wearing the raiment of disbelief, with sin and disobedience causing him to become completely worthless and insignificant in the sight of Allah ﷻ?"[1]

"The root of all diseases of the heart is our love and attachment to this materialistic world. We know this world is temporary, yet we find it so hard to disengage from it. May the Almighty guide our hearts into desiring what is lasting—the Hereafter."[2]

---

[1] Ibn al-Qayyim, *Spiritual Disease and its Cure.*
[2] Mufti Menk, Motivational Moments Part II.

4

"The condition of one who relies on Allah ﷻ is like that of one to whom a king gave a dirham, then it was stolen from him; then the King said to him: 'I have several times more, so do not worry. When you come to me, I will give you more of my treasures than that.' So, if (that person) knows the truth of the king's statement, trusts him, and knows his treasures are full of it, then what he missed will not make him sad."[1]

Therefore, Allah ﷻ guarantees guidance for anyone seeking it. Allah ﷻ will never turn down the dua [supplication] of guidance from any of His servants. Therefore, just as the man trusted that the king would give him more, the trust in Allah ﷻ to reform our hearts and faith should be as strong. As Shaykh al-Islam Ibn Taymiyyah رَحَمَهُاللّٰه says: "Putting one's trust and faith in Allah ﷻ is more general than just putting one's trust in Allah ﷻ for worldly interests. The real *mutawakkil* [the one who places their trust in Allah ﷻ] is the person who puts his faith in Allah ﷻ, hoping to reform his heart and faith, and to protect his tongue and will, which is why he invokes Allah ﷻ in every prayer and says, "You [Alone] we worship and from You [Alone] we seek help."[2]

In order to put your trust in Allah ﷻ we have to know Him first. He is *al-Ṣamad* as described in Surat al-Ikhlāṣ: "[It] means the one you turn to when you have a need, and you are never disappointed. He has everything you need. He is the one who becomes your goal. He is the one you will always need, and He will always have what you need, and He will need no one or anything. Allah ﷻ knows everything about

---

[1] Ibn al-Qayyim.
[2] Ibn Taymiyyah.

every situation (knows the inside and outside of every circumstance and situation whether you are aware or not aware) and thus no one can fulfill those needs better than Him. He is forbearing and caring; head—highest authority after which there is no higher authority than Him and here you have connection with the highest of the high directly; maker of all things; sought after whenever you desire something but also the one you need in desperate situations. The purpose of dua is to fill you and fulfill you. Allah ﷻ will always give you what you need and will never disappoint you, contentment results from this."[1]

---

[1] Bayyinah, Deeper Look Surah Ikhlās.

5

Ibn Qayyim al-Jawziyyah رحمه الله summarizes trust in Allah ﷻ very beautifully, in observing that there are three ways or levels to trust Allah ﷻ. He says the first level of trust in Allah ﷻ is the way that we would trust an agent (*wakīl*). When we trust an agent then the agent is still in service to us, we are not in service to the agent. We give the agent instructions and when the agent does not do exactly what we tell him or her to do, we lose trust in that agent, and we try to replace them. Allah ﷻ is not going to be this type of *wakīl* for us, we must move our concept of Him to a higher level.

The second level of trust is the type that a child has for its mother. A child goes to its mother knowing that no one loves it more than her and no one offers it a greater sense of comfort; so even if she punishes the child and it cries and has a tantrum, it still goes back to its mother for comfort because the child trusts its mother's love and knows she has its best interests at heart even when she punishes her child.

He explained the third level of trust in Allah ﷻ as being like the trust a dead person being washed has for those washing him. That is an absolute state of trust in Allah ﷻ; complete trust that He will not move us in a direction out of hatred, or in a direction that is not in our best interests, complete trust that He will maintain our affairs and see us through every difficulty, and that every difficulty is meant for us to gain a further perspective and further closeness to Him on the path to His love. This highest level of trust in our relationship with

Allah ﷻ allows us to focus on His love for us. Where there is mistrust, there cannot be true love."[1]

The love, care, and mercy that Allah ﷻ has for us surpasses infinitely what our mothers, fathers, brothers, sisters, and friends can ever have for us. Only then, by trusting Allah ﷻ to want your best interests and to take care of your affairs, does it become easy to live. Allah ﷻ constantly makes you return to Him in different ways so that you may enter the house that was made for you in Paradise. That house belongs to you, so do not lose it. Trust Allah ﷻ and He will move mountains for you.

[1] Omar Suleiman, *Allah Loves*, pp. 43-44.

6

Ibn Taymiyyah رَحِمَهُاللَّه said, "Even if it attains all that it can enjoy of created things, it will not feel at peace or find tranquility, because it has an inherent need for its Lord, for He is the focus of its worship, love and seeking, and this is the only way to attain joy, happiness, pleasure, peace and tranquility.

For if a person is helped to attain what he loves, seeks, desires and wants, but he does not worship Allah ﷻ, he will never achieve anything but sorrow, regret, and suffering. He can never be free of the pain and hardship of this life except through loving Allah ﷻ sincerely, so that Allah ﷻ becomes his ultimate desire and he loves Him for what He is, and he loves anyone or anything else only for His sake, and he does not love anything for its own sake except Allah ﷻ."

Ibn Taymiyyah explains that happiness and fulfilment can only be attained by being true slaves of Allah ﷻ. Feelings of unhappiness, misery and dissatisfaction come from being alienated and far away from Allah ﷻ, not because of the lack of some of our material needs and wants. Happiness and fulfilment, both in this world and the Hereafter, can be achieved only through drawing close to Allah ﷻ and worshipping Him.[1]

---

[1] Ibn Taymiyyah.

7

I would give up my kingdom to be like Sālim

Ibn Kathīr رحمه الله said: "The Umayyad Caliph Hishām bin Abdul Malik performed Hajj. While he was performing *ṭawāf* around the House [the Ka'bah] he saw Sālim bin 'Abdullāh bin 'Umar bin al-Khaṭṭāb.

Sālim was carrying his broken shoes in his hand, and he was wearing a garment that was not worth two dirhams [the currency of that time]. The Caliph Hishām went close to him and said, "O Sālim, do you need anything?" Sālim looked at him with surprise and anger. Then he said to him, "Are you not embarrassed, while we are in the house of Allah ﷻ, you want me to ask other than Allah ﷻ for my needs?" Severe embarrassment and shame appeared on the face of the Caliph Hishām, and he left Sālim alone and completed his *ṭawāf*, but he continued to watch him.

When he saw Sālim outside of Masjid al-Ḥarām, he caught up with him and said, "O Sālim, you refused to tell me what you needed inside of Masjid al-Ḥarām, so ask me now since you are outside of the Masjid.' Sālim said to him, "Should I ask you for my worldly need or my needs in the Hereafter?" The Caliph said to him, "O Salim, ask me for your worldly needs, as for needs in the Hereafter, you only ask Allah ﷻ for those." Sālim said, "O Hishām, I swear by Allah ﷻ, I have not asked for any worldly needs from the One who owns the world, so how could I ask of someone who does not own it?" The Caliph Hishām's eyes filled with tears, and he said his famous statement, "I would give my entire kingdom to be like Sālim.'"[1]

"And your Lord says: 'Call upon Me, I will answer you.'" [From the Quran, 40:60]

The Prophet ﷺ said, "Verily your Lord is Generous and Shy. If His servant raises his hands to Him [in supplication], He becomes shy to return them empty."[2]

Having a generous, loving Master who loves to listen to us speaking with Him and hear our voices, what more can we ask for? He hears every dua, every wish we did not even verbalize, and He answers them all in a way that will get us to Paradise.

[1] *Al-Bidāyah wa-l-Nihāyah* (9/235), translated by Rasheed ibn Estes Barbee.
[2] Narrated in Aḥmad, Abū Dawūd, and al-Tirmidhī.

8

Ibn al-Qayyim رَحِمَهُ اللّٰه said: "It was from His mercy that He blemished their worldly life for them and made it imperfect. This was so they would not feel comfortable in it nor feel secure regarding it, and so they would aspire for the endless enjoyment in His abode and in His company. So, in reality, He deprived them so that He would give to them, and He tried them so that He would relieve them, and He put them to death so that He would give them [everlasting] life."[1]

Imam al-Ghazālī رَحِمَهُ اللّٰه said "If you see Allah ﷻ, Mighty and Magnificent, holding back this world from you, frequently trying you with adversity and tribulation, know that you hold a great status with Him. Know that He is dealing with you as He does with His *awliyā'* [saints] and chosen elite and is watching over you."

Yaḥyā bin Muʿādh رَحِمَهُ اللّٰه said: "The world is worthless to its Lord, and yet it belongs to Him. So, it is not right that you value it so much when it is not even yours."[2]

---

[1] Ibn al-Qayyim, *Ighāthat al-Lahfān*.
[2] *Ḥilyat al-Awliyā'*, 14549.

9

Imam Aḥmad رَحِمَهُ اللهُ said: "I worshipped Allah ﷻ for fifty years and I did not experience the sweetness of worship until I abandoned three things:

1. I abandoned pleasing the people in order to be able to speak the truth.

2. I abandoned the companionship of sinners until I found companionship of the righteous.

3. I abandoned the sweetness of the worldly life until I found the sweetness of [seeking after] the Hereafter."[1]

Ibn al-Qayyim رَحِمَهُ اللهُ said: "if you insist on mixing with people and exposing yourself to desires while wishing to rectify your heart, then you have indeed sought the impossible!"[2]

Al-Ḥasan al-Baṣrī رَحِمَهُ اللهُ said: "When I was born, I was born alone, and when I shall die I will die alone. When I am placed in my grave I will be alone, and when I am taken to account before Allah ﷻ, I shall be alone. If I then enter the Fire it will be alone. And if I enter Paradise, it will be alone. So, what business do I have with people?"

---

[1] *Siyar Aʿlām al-Nubalāʾ*, 11/34.
[2] Ibn al-Qayyim, *Captured Thoughts*, p. 129.

10

True Fear of Allah ﷻ Results in all Good

Ibn al-Jawzī رحمه الله said: "My son, when fear of Allah ﷻ is real, you shall see all good. A person who truly fears his Lord does not worry about others and does not put himself in a position where his religion is at risk. Whoever takes care of Allah's ﷻ limits shall be taken care of by Him."[1]

Allah's Messenger ﷺ said to Ibn ʿAbbās ؓ: "Safeguard Allah ﷻ and He will safeguard you. Safeguard Allah ﷻ and you will find Him in front of you."[2]

The reality of remembrance and fear of Allah ﷻ

It is reported that Saʿīd b. Jubayr رحمه الله said: "Verily, fear (*al-khashyah*) is that you fear Allah ﷻ such that your fear comes between you and your disobedience [of Allah ﷻ]. That is *al-khashyah*. And *dhikr* [remembrance] is obedience to Allah ﷻ: whoever obeys Allah has remembered Him; and whoever does not obey Him is not a rememberer of Him, even if he says much *tasbīḥ* and recites much Quran."[3]

---

[1] Ibn al-Jawzī, *Sincere Counsel to the Students of Sacred Knowledge*, p. 72.
[2] Hadith 19, *40 Ḥadīth of al-Nawawī*.
[3] Al-Dhahabī, *Siyar Aʿlām al-Nubalāʾ*, 4:326.

II

Ibn al-Jawzī رحمه الله said to his son in regards to awakening after heedlessness: "My son, do not let your past carelessness make you lose hope of achieving good, for many people have come back to wakefulness after long sleep."[1]

The power of Lā ilāha illa 'llāh:

Prophet Mūsā عليه السلام said to Allah جل جلاله, "Lord, teach me something by which I can remember you and invoke you." Allah جل جلاله replied, "O Mūsā, say: *Lā ilāha illa 'llāh!*" Mūsā عليه السلام said, "Lord, but all Your servants say this!" Allah جل جلاله repeated, "Say: *Lā ilāha illa 'llāh!*" Mūsā عليه السلام replied, "I wish for something specific for myself." Allah جل جلاله said, "O Mūsā, were the seven heavens and everything they contain besides Me, and the seven earths placed on one side of a scale, and '*Lā ilāha illa 'llāh*' on the other, it would outweigh the former."[2]

Allah جل جلاله has saved you before, aided you before, and eased your heart; He will surely do it again just as He did all the previous times. Imam al-Shāfi'ī رحمه الله said, "The Lord who has taken care of you till today, will He not manage your affairs in the future?"

Ibn al-Jawzī رحمه الله said, "If you had piety, nothing of what you seek would be difficult to attain, because the key of piety opens every door. When the pious person [who fears Allah جل جلاله] settles himself down with pure piety, he shall never be harmed. On the other hand, when he

[1] Ibn al-Jawzī, *Sincere Counsel to the Students of Sacred Knowledge*, p. 56.
[2] *Ṣaḥīḥ Ibn Ḥibbān*, no. 6218.

deviates from piety, then he shall encounter nothing but distress and aggravation. You are the most precious creature to Allah ﷻ, so be content with what Allah ﷻ has decreed for you, because he who loves never questions or accuses the one he loves. The Grace of Allah ﷻ upon you in all that He has created for your sake is as clear as daylight, so how could you imagine that He would neglect you when you are at the root of it all?

Observe the kindness and compassion of Allah ﷻ; He inspires ants to store food and inspires them to break the seed before storing it, so that it does not grow afterwards; He inspires them to break the seed of coriander into four quarters, because if it was broken into only two halves it would continue to grow. To see a spider while it builds its house is to witness craftsmanship that would dazzle and confound the architects."[1]

[1] Ibn al-Jawzī, *Seeds of Admonishment and Reform* pp. 185-187.

12

A reminder in case you ever forget:

A wise person said: "Remind yourself that your only right in this world is what Allah ﷻ has decreed for you, and that worrying will not change that.

Remember that work (doing good and constantly aiming to make oneself better) is something you must do regardless of what you think Allah ﷻ has decreed for you, lest you be complacent and sit and wait for it, because Allah ﷻ provides to those who work hard. Remember that what you think is good for you may not be good for you in Allah's ﷻ eyes.

Remember that Allah ﷻ always does what is a blessing for you so not getting what you expect is still the best blessing for you.

Remember that Allah ﷻ has placed you in *this* time and *this* place and put you under *this* pressure and in *this* situation (where *this* means every single one) to learn from it and get closer to Allah ﷻ and closer to the Straight Path, even if you do not see it.

Remember that if you do not get what you have been looking for, Allah ﷻ has answered your prayers for something better.

Remember that if you do not get what you were asking for, it could be that you are not ready yet for it.

Remember that if Allah ﷻ gives you responsibility and power, that you are responsible for using that power and responsibility in ways that would benefit and not harm yourself or others.

Remember that being prevented from something could be to prevent it from you: its danger, its seduction to bad actions, or its pulling you from more beneficial actions.

Remember that Allah ﷻ loves you so trust Him, and He is watching you so fear Him. Do not despair if you fail, for you will have not failed anything in Allah's ﷻ eyes. And do not be excessively happy if you pass, for Allah ﷻ will test you using that responsibility."

13

When speaking about worldly pursuits, the Qur'an uses the term, "walk".

When speaking about our journey to prayer, it uses the term, "proceed".

When speaking about our pursuit of Paradise, it uses the expression "Race!"

But, when speaking about our pursuit of Allah ﷻ, it uses the term, "Flee!" [i.e., flee towards Allah]. Different ambitions deserve different levels of enthusiasm. Allah ﷻ is the greatest ambition. Are your priorities in life a reflection of the above? Priorities in our daily life determine what receives our attention and what does not.

Ibn al-Jawzī رَحِمَهُ اللهُ warns against not setting our priorities in order, "O hermit of this monastery, has any traveling caravan passed by you? How sad it is for one whose regret is of benefit for him no longer! This is because hands of idleness and languor manipulated his time; thus, he ended up lost, and the palms of old age broke apart the handhold of his youth, and thus he ended up ruined.

O you who pray at night, kindly intercede for those who spend their nights in slumber; O you whose heart is alive. be so kind as to ask for the mercy of Allah ﷻ to be bestowed upon the one whose heart is dead; O you, the ambassadors of endeavor, kindly deliver the letters of the distressed."[1]

---

[1] Ibn al-Jawzī, *Seeds of Admonishment and Reform*, p. 195.

14

Shaykh Semir, may Allah be pleased with him, said, "When you lose your desperation toward Allah ﷻ, that is the problem. Your reliance must always be on Allah ﷻ. You lose that sweetness of faith you have with Allah ﷻ when you lose your desperation toward Him. To rely on Allah ﷻ is to seek Him in every aspect of your life, including protection."

Nouman Ali Khan said: "Sometimes Allah ﷻ will put you in an extremely, extremely, extremely difficult position in your life. He will put you in an incredibly difficult position and then he will ask you to trust Me and I will bring whatever good is there back to you but you have to let it go and you just have to trust Me. Why does Allah ﷻ, wait for us to ask Him? Because Allah ﷻ wants you to show desperation. You have to realize you cannot overcome it alone. Having [the illusion that you can overcome it alone] is more of a calamity than anything—it is arrogance. You [have] to ask with desperation. For one to beg Allah ﷻ to salvage him and save him from this calamity.

You will be pulled by shaytan to sin in small steps which in and of themselves are small and not noticeable. [Shaytan] relies on you not noticing because once you do, he backs away. Every step you follow, he will increase the level of the sin gradually until it is out of control."

15

It is reported that a man once went to Ibrāhīm b. Adham and said, "O Abū Isḥāq, I continually wrong my own self, and I turn away from everything that invites me to improve my way of life." Ibrāhīm said, "If you can fulfil five conditions, then sinning will never harm you, and you can fulfil your desires as much as you want."

The man exclaimed, "Tell me those conditions!"

Ibrāhīm said, "As for the first, if you want to disobey Allah ﷻ, then do not eat from His sustenance."

The man said, "What then will I eat, for everything on the earth is from His sustenance?"

Ibrāhīm said, "Listen! Are you being sensible when you eat from His sustenance while you are disobedient to Him?"

The man said, "No. What is the second condition?"

Ibrāhīm said, "If you want to disobey Allah ﷻ, then do not live in any of His lands."

The man said, "This is even worse than the first. All that is in the East and West belong to Him. So where then will I live?"

Ibrāhīm said, "Listen! If you insist on disobeying Him while you eat from His sustenance and live in His lands, then at least look for some spot where He cannot see you and disobey Him there."

The man exclaimed, "O Ibrāhīm! How can I do that, when He even knows the deepest secrets that are in the breasts of men? What is the fourth condition?" he asked desperately.

Ibrāhīm said, "When the angel of death comes to take your soul, then say to him, 'Give me some respite, so that I can repent sincerely and perform good deeds.'"

The man said, "When the time comes, the angel will not accept that plea from me."

Ibrāhīm said, "Listen! If you cannot put off death in order to repent, then how do you expect to be saved?"

The man asked, "Tell me the fifth condition."

Ibrāhīm said, "When the guardians of the Hellfire come to take you away on the Day of Resurrection, do not go with them"

The man exclaimed, "But they will not release me!"

Ibrāhīm asked, "Then how do you expect to be saved?"

The man replied, "Stop, stop! That is enough for me. I ask Allah ﷻ to forgive me, and I indeed repent to Him."

The man then dedicated his life to the worship of Allah ﷻ from that day.

16

"If the state of [Prophet] Adam ﷺ was expressed in words, it would say, O Lord, you have captured those who love You, and so I seek your Mercy, for I am a pot that is meant to break, and because of that it was handed to a shaky hand; and You have said, 'If you have not sinned I would have replaced you with people who would commit sin and seek forgiveness.'¹ He wept for the loss of his house (Paradise) once, and a thousand times for losing the Neighbor (Allah ﷻ), for indeed departure disturbs and distance agitates."²

For everything you lose there is a replacement, but the one who loses Allah ﷻ will never find anything to replace Him with.

---

¹ *Ṣaḥīḥ Muslim*, no. 2749.
² Ibn al-Jawzī, *Seeds of Admonishment and Reform*, pp. 34-37.

17

O Allah ﷻ, make me an instrument of Your peace.
Where there is hatred, let me bring love.
Where there is offense, let me bring pardon.
Where there is discord, let me bring union.
Where there is error, let me bring truth.
Where there is doubt, let me bring faith.
Where there is despair, let me bring hope.
Where there is darkness, let me bring Your light.
Where there is sadness, let me bring joy.
O Allah ﷻ, let me not seek as much
to be consoled as to console,
to be understood as to understand,
to be loved as to love,
for it is in giving that one receives,
it is in self-forgetting that one finds,
it is in pardoning that one is pardoned,
it is in dying that one is raised to eternal life.[1]

---

[1] This anonymous prayer is often credited to St. Francis of Assisi but has been traced
to Father Esther Bouquerel who first published it in his journal in 1912 (the word
"Lord" has been replaced with "Allah").

18

Shaykh al-Shaʻrāwī رحمه الله said, "Allah ﷻ said: 'O son of Adam do not be afraid of any power or sovereignty as long as My sovereignty remains, and My sovereignty never ceases. O son of Adam do not fear tightened sustenance as long as My storehouses are full, and My storehouses are never empty. O son of Adam I created you to worship so do not play, I have already set your share of sustenance so do not make yourself tired.'

He does not mean tiring your limbs. Rather, do not tire your heart with worry. Your limbs work while your heart puts its trust in Allah ﷻ. 'I created you to worship so do not play and I guaranteed your sustenance so do not make yourself tired. I swear by My Glory and Might if you are content with what I have allocated for you, I will bring comfort to your heart and body, and you will be praised by Me. On the other hand if you are not content with what I have allocated for you, I swear by My glory and Might I will let the world loose on you where you will run just like animals run in the wild and you will still not get more than what I originally allocated for you.

O son of Adam I created the sevens heavens and earth effortlessly so would it trouble Me to simply send a loaf of bread your way? O son of Adam do not ask for tomorrow's sustenance just like I have not asked you for tomorrow's deeds. O son of Adam I love you. So, by my rights over you, love Me.'"

As the poet said: "He who wears the robe of contentedness will surely be rich even in poverty and will find richness even in a place of aridity."

19

Shaykh Wassim Yousif said: "The questioner asks where can I find happiness. O brother, your question is great. Where is happiness? Look at this body, it is created from clay... clear? However you take of care of it or comfort it, the soul still remains trapped in it, correct?

You with your body can move anywhere. The body remains clay with the soul inside of it. The happiness of the body is not like that of the soul at all. The happiness of the body comes from food, among other things. The soul has a separate world, the world of the Unseen. It does not get satisfied except with closeness of the One who created it, Allah ﷻ. Therefore, you cannot ignore either of them. Shaykh ibn Uthaymīn رحمه الله said the more luxury you give the body, the more the soul becomes depressed, no doubt. You must give it its portion of happiness which is closeness to Allah ﷻ. Whoever does good will be rewarded with contentment. 'Whoever does righteousness whether male or female while he or she is a believer, We will grant him a good life.'[1] Why did Allah ﷻ not say 'a happy life'? Because this world has no happiness in it and its happiness is not complete. Why a good life? Because you might get moments of sadness, but your soul gets relieved when you say there is no might or power except with Allah ﷻ."

[1] The Quran, verse 16:97.

20

Ibn al-Qayyim رَحِمَهُ اللهُ says: "The word *al-Rabb* can only ever be applied to Allah ﷻ.[1] It is one of the Names of Allah ﷻ and means the One who nurtures and sustains all His servants through regulating the affairs and granting all kinds of favors and blessings. More specifically, He is the One who nurtures and sustains His sincere friends by correcting and purifying their hearts, souls, and manners. This is why their supplications are frequently made with this Noble Name, because they seek this specific nurturing. Al-Saʿdī said, "The Lord is the One who nourishes and sustains the whole of creation, meaning everything aside from Allah ﷻ, by the very fact of His creating them, His preparing for them all that they need and His favoring them with great blessings, which if removed would also remove any possibility of the creation surviving. Therefore, every blessing they possess is from Him, exalted is He.

His sustaining His creation is of two types: General and Specific. As for the general, it is His creating the creation, granting them provisions, and guiding them to that which would benefit them to have them survive in this world. As for the specific, it is His sustaining His friends with faith and making them conform to it, perfecting and completing it for them, repressing all that would make them turn away from it, bridling any hindering factors that may be set up between them and Him, and safeguarding them from all evil.

It is possible that the reason behind the fact that most of the supplications made by the Prophets employed the word 'Lord' [*Rabb*]

---

[1] Al-Qurṭubī, vol. 1, p. 96; Ibn Kathīr, vol. 1, p. 45; al-Shawkānī, vol. 1, p. 21; al-Ālūsī, vol. 1, p. 105.

was due to it carrying this meaning, for indeed all the things they desired through their supplications fell under His Specific Lordship."[1]

"No matter what is happening in your life right now, no matter how bleak things look, anything is possible as long as you seek the Almighty with a sincere heart. He will make things happen which your limited mind could never comprehend. He will respond, and that is His Promise."[2]

Optimism is a necessary mindset for the believer. Nothing is impossible for the Almighty. He can change your condition in the blink of an eye. Show optimism by refusing to stop asking Him and always assuming the best.[3]

[1] Ibn al-Qayyim, *Spiritual Disease and Its Cure*.
[2] Mufti Menk, Motivational Moments Part II
[3] Abas Idris.

21

Abū Kabshah al-Anmārī 🙵 narrated that the Messenger of Allah 🪷 said: "There are three things for which I swear and narrate to you about, so remember it." He said: "The wealth of a slave [of Allah 🕮] shall not be decreased by charity, no slave [of Allah 🕮] suffers injustice and is patient with it except that Allah adds to his honor; no slave [of Allah 🕮] opens up a door to begging except that Allah opens a door for him to poverty"—or a statement similar—"And I shall narrate to you a narration, so remember it." He said: "The world is only for four persons:

1. A slave whom Allah provides with wealth and knowledge, so he has *taqwā* of his Lord with it, nurtures the ties of kinship with it, and he knows that Allah has a right in it [i.e., his wealth]. So, this is the most virtuous rank.

2. And a slave whom Allah provides with knowledge, but He does not provide with wealth. So, he has a truthful intent, saying: 'If I had wealth, then I would do the deeds of so-and-so with it.' He has his intention, so their rewards are the same.

3. And a slave whom Allah provides with wealth, but He does not provide with knowledge. [So, he] spends his wealth rashly without knowledge, nor having *taqwā* of his Lord, nor nurturing the ties of kinship, and he does not know that Allah has a right in it. So, this is the most despicable rank.

4. And a slave whom Allah does not provide with wealth nor knowledge, so he says: 'If I had wealth, then I would do the

deeds of so-and-so with it.' He has his intention, so their sin is the same."[1]

"Secret charity is enough to turn a road filled with thorns into a bed full of scented roses."[2]

[1] *Jāmiʿ al-Tirmidhī*, no. 2325.
[2] Thauheeda Thameem.

22

Ibn al-Qayyim رَحِمَهُ اللهُ wrote a very powerful point on the idea of prayer, saying that "When a servant of Allah enters into the prayer, then he turns away from Allah ﷻ. This is not a physical turning away from Allah but an internal turning away from Him. Allah ﷻ says to the servant, 'O my servant, where are you turning to that is better than Me? Have you found something better than Me? More worthy than Me?'"[1] Whenever we supplicate to Allah ﷻ to gain something for ourselves, it means we are not seeking Him, we are seeking something *from* Him.

Ibn al-Jawzī رَحِمَهُ اللهُ said "Paradise is given to you in trade for worldly detachment and asceticism [i.e. removing the love of this worldly life from your heart]; Hell is kept away from you if you abandon [the temptation of] this worldly life; love cannot convince of its sincerity unless it is inscribed into the soul, because the authority of love never accepts bribes.

O you who seeks his Lord, detach yourself from the love of yourself, for your heart is too fragile and weak to have your Lord and yourself therein at the same time; it is either to keep Allah by Himself or yourself alone; and when you forget your love for yourself, only then will you find Allah in your heart. When Ibrāhīm was in a state of rigorous self-denial, his strength manifested itself the day he said "I have nothing to request from you." Indeed, it was a journey at which the feet of contentment walked across the land of longing. As the poets said:

---

[1] Omar Suleiman, *Allah Loves*, pp. 113-114.

*I visited you as I was longing for you, but even if the land had been
full of embers I would still have walked on it to reach you*

*If the ember of yearning is blazing in my heart.
Our meeting shall be the water by which you shall extinguish it.*

*They wonder at a heart that longs for agony;
they are unaware that in reality it is sweeter than honey.*

When knowledge [and the Quran] is rooted in the heart, all calamities
become bearable."[1]

[1] Ibn al-Jawzī, *Seeds of Admonishment and Reform*, pp. 117-120.

23

A phonebook with the contacts you need

Allah ﷻ speaks to you in each of verses below. Allah ﷻ understands your state but still wants to listen to your voice calling Him.

When we call someone, they can only hear what comes from our tongues but cannot know the state of our hearts. But what about when we say Allah ﷻ knows? Allah ﷻ knows what is in your heart. More than that, He wants to hear you say it to Him and there is no slave that raises his hands towards Allah ﷻ except that Allah will fill their hands with something they asked or that which is better.

The Prophet ﷺ said, "Verily your Lord is Generous and Shy. If His servant raises his hands to Him [in supplication] He becomes shy to return them empty."[1]

Feeling Sad	Quran 2:25
Having made a Mistake	Quran 39:53
Wanting Peace	Quran 5:16
Wanting a Friend	Quran 2:257
Feel Discriminated Against	Quran 33:35
Facing Racism	Quran 49:13

[1] *Sunan Abī Dawūd*, no. 1488. Graded ṣaḥīḥ.

Seeking Love & Tranquility	Quran 30:21
Feeling Depressed	Quran 13:28
Wanting a Soul Mate	Quran 50:16
Feeling Not Appreciated	Quran 76:22
Feeling that Nothing is Going Right	Quran 12:87
Feeling Under-privileged	Quran 14:34
Feeling Tired of Hardships	Quran 94:05
Someone Picking a Fight with You	Quran 2:62
Wanting Forgiveness	Quran 3:135
Wanting Assurance	Quran 15:49

Ibn Taymiyyah رحمه الله said: "Trials and tribulations are like feeling the heat and cold, when one knows that they cannot be avoided, he will not feel anger at their onset, nor will he be distressed or disheartened."[1]

---

[1] Ibn al-Qayyim, *Al-Madārij*, 3/289.

24

"When you find yourself incapable, ask The Benefactor, and when you feel indolent, turn to the Giver of opportunity. You will only achieve good by obeying Him, and no good will bypass you except due to your disobedience. Have you not seen that the disobedient never succeed or achieve their goals!

Have you not heard the poet say:

'By Allah, never have I come to visit You
Except that the earth compacted (flattened) before me.

I have never resolved to leave Your door
Except that I tripped over my garment's tail.'[1][2]

The Messenger of Allah ﷺ narrated that Allah ﷻ said: "When My servant draws close to Me by the span of a palm, I draw close to him by the cubit. And when he draws close to Me by the cubit, I draw close to him by [the space covered by] two arm spans. And when he comes to me walking, I rush [run] towards him."[3]

A cubit is the length of the forearm which is almost three times the size of a span of a palm. An arm span is the measurement of one arm from fingertips to the other arm's fingertips when raised to the sides. So, Allah ﷻ will draw to you by not just one arm span but two which

---

[1] *Siyar A'lām al-Nubalā'*, 21/58, said to be poetry of al-Murtaḍā, the father of al-Imām Abū l-Faḍā'il Muḥammad b. 'Abdullāh b. al-Qāsim b. Muẓfir al-Shāfi'ī with "yā layl" in the place of Allah.
[2] Ibn al-Jawzī, *Sincere Counsel to the Seekers of True Knowledge*, pp. 40-41.
[3] *Ṣaḥīḥ Muslim*, no. 2675a.

is much more than 7 times the size of a cubit. Wonder at Allah's ﷻ love and care for you.

25

A wise person wrote this poem:

Allah ﷻ is the All-Merciful Master we have who will welcome you with
Come here
Welcome back
I will keep you safe
I will keep you warm
Let Me hold your worries
Let Me heal you
I love you
I have so much for you
I am not mad at you
Trust me
I will never abandon you
My grace will never run out
Remember with Me

26

Allah ﷻ says:

"If you support Allah, He will support you," [The Quran, 47:7]

and

"Remember Me and I shall remember you," [The Quran, 2:152]

and

"Fulfill My covenant and I shall fulfill yours." [The Quran, 2:40]

"When all you see are shadows and darkness, know that the light you need is in your heart. The Almighty illuminates a way out beyond anything you could have planned or imagined."[1]

"It is not strange that I love You because I am a weak servant, but it is strange that You love me when You are the King of Kings."[2]

[1] Farah Ahmed.
[2] Sara Seedat.

27

The Quickest way to draw closer to Allah according to Imam Ibn al-Qayyim رَحَمَهُ اللهُ

"Condemning oneself [with strict self-accounting] is the practice of the truthful servants of Allah ﷻ. A servant would draw closer to Allah ﷻ in a moment of self-accounting much more than he would through his or her actions."

Your purpose in this life is to increase the goodness within yourself, and in so doing, to become close to Allah ﷻ. Because Allah ﷻ only allows near Him those who are pure and good! And this closeness to Him is in proportion to the degree to which one is pure and the degree of goodness an individual has within him or her. This process of eliminating evil within oneself (self-purification) and the increasing of goodness is called *tazkiyah*. And *tazkiyah* is not possible unless one takes account of oneself very strictly, to discover what evil things need to be purified from one's soul, and what good traits need to be further developed.

He should be strict in this self- accounting just as traders in this world are very strict when they do accounts with their partners at the end of every business period. What is meant by self-accounting is that one should look at his capital and his profits and losses, so that he may see, at the end of the day, whether he is gaining or losing.

In spiritual terms, his capital is the obligatory duties he owes to Allah ﷻ or those obligatory duties he owes to his fellow humans; his profit is where he did non-obligatory good deeds towards Allah ﷻ or his fellow humans; and his loss is the sins resulting from either transgressing the rights of Allah ﷻ or the rights of people. So let him take account, first, of obligatory duties, and if he commits a sin, let him impose on himself some sort of penance, to make up for his heedlessness.

He should take stock of himself with every breath he takes, with every sin of the body and also every sin of the heart [i.e., thoughts, feelings, and emotions] at every moment of his day. SubhanAllah, if a man was to throw a stone into his house for every sin he commits, his house would be filled up to its ceiling within a very short period. But he does not pay much attention to remembering his sins, although they have already been recorded against him, and they shall never be forgotten:

"Allah has kept account of it, while they have forgotten it." [The Quran, 58:6].

Understanding the laws set by Allah ﷻ governing goodness and wickedness are the first steps in realizing that every action has a consequence. Ibn al-Qayyim رحمه الله explains: "The origin of goodness is to know that whatever Allah ﷻ wills will be, and whatever He does not will, will not be. Then you will be sure that good deeds are blessings from Allah ﷻ and you will praise Allah ﷻ for them and invoke Him not to prevent you from them. You will know that sins are punishments, so you will invoke Him to protect you from committing sins and not to leave you with your own doings either good or bad. Those who know best agree that the origin of goodness is aid from Allah ﷻ, and that the origin of wickedness is being deserted by Allah ﷻ. And they agree that aid is when one is not abandoned by Allah ﷻ and left to his own devices. So if every good is aid from Allah ﷻ and has nothing to do with the servant, then its key is supplication—resorting to Allah ﷻ, and sincerely desiring to please Him. Whenever the servant is given this key, he will be welcomed, and if the servant loses this key, the door to goodness will be closed on him."[1]

May Allah ﷻ never allow this door to close on us. O Allah ﷻ, I beg forgiveness for sins which I have repeated after having repented from them before You; I beg forgiveness for all the promises which I have made to You on my behalf and then did not fulfill; I beg forgiveness for Your gift from which I drew strength only to use it in Your disobedience; I beg forgiveness for all those good actions that I intended for Your sake only, but later mixed other motives in them; I beg You for deeds that will be accepted, knowledge that will lead to success, efforts that will be appreciated, and a business that will never fail; O Allah ﷻ, do not humiliate me as You have full Knowledge of me and do not punish me as You have all Power over me; I beg You for a truthful tongue and a return to You which is neither humiliating nor disgracing. Ameen. It is for us to supplicate, and for You to accept; this is my effort, and my reliance is on You.

It was reported that one of our Pious Predecessors, Tawbah ibn al-Summah رحمه الله was known to take strict account of himself. One day, when he was doing that, he realized that he was 60 years old. He worked out the number of days of his life and realized that it was 21,500 days. He screamed and said, "Woe is me! Am I going to meet the Sovereign with 21,500 sins? How about if there were 10,000 sins every day?" And with this reflection he fell down dead! "How quickly he was taken to al-Firdaws al-A'lā."

---

[1] Ibn al-Qayyim, *al-Fawā'id*.

28

You are not dealing with anyone comparable to Him. His forgiveness is beyond imagination. His generosity is unrestricted. The more you ask of Him, the more you please Him, and if you were to ask Him for every little thing until your heart and imagination are exhausted, you would not have taken from His kingdom anything. But do not ever stop asking Him, and do not ever sever your connection with Him. And if you are ever distant from Him, then it is only because you moved."[1]

The Prophet ﷺ said: "ask Allah (ﷻ) from His bounty because you have a Master that loves to be asked"

Omar Suleiman may Allah ﷻ reward him wrote: "Anytime we show kindness to someone, Allah ﷻ will never allow us to show more kindness to someone else than Allah ﷻ will show to us. The most beloved people to Allah ﷻ are the ones who are most beneficial to people because Allah ﷻ sees them as a vehicle, Allah uses them as a part of carrying out that relief in other people's lives."[2]

"Whatever good you do will come back to you in one way or another. When you help someone else go higher in life, the Almighty will send someone to help you go higher. Good begets good. That's how it works! Keep doing good. Don't lose your values because of the misdeeds of others. Inspire as many as you can to do the same. It will change lives. The more you give, the more you'll get back. Even if it's

[1] Ammar Al-Shukry's reflection.
[2] Omar Suleiman, *Allah Loves*, pp. 59-60.

not money, give your time, words, and advice. He will reward you in greater ways!"[1]

"In this world, a man finds in the remembrance of Allah, praising Him and worshipping Him, a delight that is incomparable to anything else"[2]

---

[1] Mufti Menk, Motivational Moments II.
[2] Ibn Taymiyyah, Minhāj al-Sunnah, 5/389.

29

"Allah ﷻ took two things out of my hands. The past and the future. The scars, mistakes, regrets, choices, and failures of the past cannot be undone. The future, as much as I like to think I have a plan for, is entirely out of my hands. But Allah ﷻ gave me the gift and the responsibility of the present. So how do I make the most of it?

I cannot afford to let my mind waste the present by dwelling on the hurtful past or the worrisome future. You and I have wasted so much of our precious moments doing that and it has brought us nothing but more of the same.

I must use the past and future to my advantage. The past is nothing more than lessons learned. What the Quran calls *'ibrah.* The future belongs to Him, so I leave it to Him with prayer and give the today He bestowed upon me my best effort. There is plenty of time for looking back at the past and worrying about the future in our graves."[1]

Mufti Menk, may Allah ﷻ reward him, said the following[2] in regards to pressing on, being hopeful, and reminding us who Allah ﷻ is and what He does for us:

- If you keep looking back, living a life of regret, how can you expect to move forward and embrace all that the Almighty has in store for you?

[1] Nouman Ali Khan.
[2] Mufti Menk, Motivational Moments II.

- Do not let worries of the future consume you. Throw them out when they enter your mind. Ask the Almighty to give you what is best. Trust Him.

- We are all a work in progress. We are not perfect. As long as we are trying to be better than we were yesterday, that is what matters most.

- Get back up, no matter what knocks you down each time. Endure, press on and never give up. Great blessings come with great perseverance!

- Do not live a life of worry, frustration and disappointment. It saps your energy and steals your joy. You will not be able to see His blessings.

- Worry is part of life. It is natural for us as humans to have such thoughts. What is important is not to let them get the better of us.

- Learn from past experience and mistakes. The Almighty sent them for a reason. If the same situation happens again, draw on the lessons learnt.

30

"Is there any reward for goodness except goodness?" [The Quran, 55:60]

"This ayah inspired me strikingly and filled my heart with hope and tranquility. It's been in my mind from the first time it touched my heart. Such a simple yet beautiful and profound reminder it is. Whenever you feel like you were doing something good or trusted someone and got betrayed or anyone wronged you in any way, do not ever regret being good. When you do something wholeheartedly, and people don't appreciate it, always remember your goodness will not be wasted, and Allah ﷻ, the All-knower knows what you are doing. Only He can reward you justifiably, either in this world or the Hereafter.

Don't overthink before doing something good or making a change, forgiving someone, being good to someone, making someone smile even if it's a small act like saying salaam to someone. Because, whatever you do, especially to please Allah ﷻ, he will reward you with nothing but goodness, and we all know Allah's ﷻ rewards are way better than our efforts.

Also, when you try to study the Quran, don't ever think, what if you get busy or you might not be able to complete it, don't lose hope because it's never about reaching a finishing line, but the growth you made during the process. Make the best out of something you learned even if it's not much, and Allah ﷻ will reward you with more. If you're unable to leave some bad habits, adopt some good ones or be better at some other area. Always remember this ayah—you doing good will always be rewarded with good by Allah ﷻ, maybe even make that one thing easy for you what you thought was the hardest and make you among the people of the Quran."[1]

[1] Shafaque Zareen's reflection, QuranReflect.

31

Allah ﷻ loves to be loved [1]

Ibn Taymiyyah رحمه الله said: "The more the servant loves his Master, the less will he love other objects, and they will decrease in number. The less the servant loves his Master, the more he will love other objects, and they will increase in number."[2]

Ibn al-Jawzī رحمه الله said: "You who is afflicted with an ardent love for this life, although you shall never attain from it except what is decreed for you: there are many who attain provision without the least amount of effort, and there are many who expend all possible means but never receive any provision.

Plenty of good may lie concealed within what you dislike, which you would realize if only the cover over your eyes was removed. O you who seeks help for the removal of poverty by employing his complaining tongue: know that what you perceive as the prison of poverty is actually a protective fortress, and it is indeed a sickness that only nobles suffer from. Poverty is a well and neediness is its depths, whereas base desires are bonds of slavery; therefore: 'This worldly life is the prison of believers.'

It is indeed an insult to the Master when His slave asks help from someone other than Him; therefore, always ask help only from your Master. O you heedless ones, who are so focused on thinking about the means that you neglect to think of the One who creates the means and

[1] Ibn Taymiyyah, *Majmū' al-Fatāwā*, 1/54.
[2] Ibn Taymiyyah, *Majmū' al-Fatāwā*, 1/94.

causes: it is He, the one Who gives, Who can also deprive and prevent, therefore

'do not set up rivals to Allah.' [The Quran, 2: 22]" [1]

[1] Ibn al-Jawzī, *Seeds of Admonishment and Reform*, pp. 168-169.

32

Not a second passes except that Allah ﷻ the al-Ḥafīẓ (The All-Preserver, The All-Heedful, The All-Protecting) protects you.

From the beautiful book *Because You are Allah*: "Do you know that Allah ﷻ protects you every moment? Rather He protects you a thousand times every passing moment.

How?

In the moment you are reading this, you are protected by Allah ﷻ: He protects your heart from stopping, your arteries from clogging, your mind from madness, your kidneys from failing, your nerves from damage, your head from headaches, your stomach from ulcers, your intestines from colitis, your organs from paralysis, your eyes from blindness, your hearing from deafness, and your tongue from being unable to speak. You are protected every second in all these ways and many more ways (that cannot be counted)."[1]

"And He gave you from all you asked of Him. And if you should count the favors of Allah, you could not enumerate them. Indeed, mankind is [generally] most unjust and ungrateful." [The Quran, 14:34]

He protects His close friends from falling into sin, and he guards them against the plots of the shaytan so that they will be safe from his wickedness and temptations.

[1] *Li-Annaka Allāh.*

33

The life of this world is very short, and this is illustrated in the following parable: when a child is born there is the *adhān* and *iqāmah* that is recited in their ear. What usually comes shortly after the *adhān* [the call to prayer] is the *iqāmah*, followed immediately by the prayer. The life of this world is the time between the *adhān* and the *iqāmah*.

The prayer comes next. The prayer here is *Ṣalāt al-Janāzah* [the communal prayer performed over a dead person's body]. May Allah allow us to realize the dire state we are in and allow us to be aware of our time and how we spend it.

Imam ʿAlī ﷺ said, "How strange and foolish is man. He loses his health in gaining wealth. Then, to regain health he wastes his wealth. He ruins his present while worrying about his future, but weeps in the future by recalling his past. He lives as though death shall never come to him but dies in a way as if he were never born."

34

Ibn al-Qayyim ﵁ said regarding the name "Allah" ﷻ, "I cannot enumerate praise of You, You are as You have praised Yourself. How is it possible to enumerate the specificities of a Name, the object of which has every single perfection without restriction, who deserves all commendation and praise, all lauding and veneration, who possesses all magnificence and perfection, and all nobility and beauty? All goodness, beneficence, generosity, grace, and gifts belong to Him and come from Him.

This Name is not mentioned over something paltry except that it becomes plentiful, nor at a time of fear except that it removes it, nor at a time of hardship except that it lifts it, nor at a time of distress and worry except that it alleviates it, nor at a time of constraint except that it liberates it. No weak creature depends upon it except that it grants him strength, nor one undergoing humiliation except it grants him honor, nor one who is poor except that it leads him to richness, nor one who is left alone except that it grants him comfort, nor one who is overcome except that it aids him and supports him, nor one in a state of dire need except that it lifts his need, nor one who is run astray except that it draws him back.

It is the Name through which hardship is removed, through which blessings descend, through which supplications are answered, through which the foot does not slip, through which evil is repressed and good is promoted. It is the Name through which the heavens and the earth stand, because of which the heavenly scripture descended, the Messengers were sent, the laws legislated, the legal punishments established, and *jihād* legislated.

Through this Name is the creation divided into the felicitous and the wretched, and through it does the Undeniable Reality come to pass and the Final Convulsion occur. Because of it are the Scales erected, the Path laid out, and Paradise and Hell made ready. Through it is the Lord of the worlds worshipped and praised, and to establish its rights were the Messengers sent. It is about it that the questions will be asked in the grave and on the Day of Resurrection. Because of it did the dispute arise and to it one goes for judgment. Love and hate are based on it. Felicitous is one who has come to know it and establish its right, wretched is one who is ignorant of it and leaves off its right. It is the core of the creation and the command and through it do both stand and become firm, and toward it do they end."[12]

"Our Lord! You have not created all this without purpose—You are far above that!—so protect us from the torment of the Fire!" [The Quran, 3:191]

---

[1] Ibn al-Qayyim, *Spiritual Disease and its Cure*.
[2] *Fatḥ al-Majīd*, p. 15.

35

"All praise be to the One who made the different stages of life. During these stages, there are those who submit to Allah's orders and thereby advance. Others who are a wasteful of this time and thereby struck with loss and regret. Indeed, life has been designated so that people [use it] to reach the sought [i.e., Paradise] and to remove all that which causes loss and defect. Whoever lives his life appropriately [as per Allah's ﷻ commands], his life will be a trade generating for him abundantly multiplied profits, whereas the corrupt one who does not act accordingly, will find his soul ruined. A good deed is written as ten full deeds to seven hundred and more, and a sin makes the person go back to the state of disturbance he was in before."[1]

Al-Mustawrid b. Shaddād ؓ reported that the Messenger of Allah ﷺ said, "This world [i.e., its pleasures and duration] in comparison with the Hereafter is [similar to the amount of water] one gets when he puts his finger in the sea. Let him then see what it returns with."[2]

Ibn al-Qayyim رحمه الله said, "Everything that is loved, if it is not loved for His sake, then this love is nothing but distress and punishment. Every action that is not performed for His sake is wasted and severed. Every heart that does not reach Him is wretched and veiled from achieving its success and happiness. Therefore, there is nothing beyond Allah that deserves to be sought and nothing finds its conclusion with other than Him. Allah has gathered everything that could be desired from Him in His saying,

---

[1] Ibn al-Jawzī, *Awakening from the Sleep of Heedlessness.*
[2] Muslim, *Riyāḍ al-Ṣaliḥīn*, no. 462.

"There is not a single thing except that its depositories and treasures are with Us" [The Quran, 15:21]

This verse comprises a [great] treasure from the treasures [of the Quran], which is that nothing is sought except from the One who possesses its depositories and treasures, the One in whose hands lie the keys to these treasures. Seeking [things] from anyone else is seeking something from one who does not possess them or possess any authority over them, and He has gathered everything that is done for His sake in His saying,

'And that to your Lord is the final goal.'" [1] [The Quran, 53:42]

---

[1] Ibn al-Qayyim, *Spiritual Disease and its Cure.*

36

"Do not strut arrogantly about the earth: you cannot break it open, nor match the mountains in height." [The Quran, 17:37]

The noble Shaykh al-ʿAllāmah Rabīʿ b. Hādī al-Madkhalī حفظه الله said: "Wage war against yourself from falling into arrogance, an evil characteristic leading one to disbelief, belittlement of people and rejecting the truth. Humble yourself! You are a poor person; weak, created from earth, created from a sperm that is of little value, you excrete and go to the toilet many times every day, how can you be arrogant? How can you be arrogant towards the people while you are in this state? Who do you think you are? Then, if a thorn pierces you, you cry because of it, how can you be arrogant towards the people?"[1]

It is reported that Bakr b. ʿAbdullāh al-Muzanī رحمه الله said: "When you see someone older than you, say: he has preceded me in *īmān* [faith] and righteous actions, so he is better than me; and when you see someone younger than you, say: I have preceded him in sinning and disobedience, so he is better than me. And when you see your brothers honoring and revering you, say: this is a virtue they have attained; and when you see them falling short [in their treatment of you] say: this is [because of] a sin I committed."[2]

---

[1] Taken from *The Advice of Luqman the Wise to His Son*, p. 35, translated by Dr Abdullaah Lahmami.
[2] Ibn al-Jawzī, *Ṣifat al-Ṣafwah*, article 505: Bakr b. ʿAbdullāh al-Muzanī.

37

'Uthmān b. 'Affān ﷺ said: "This world is tempting, and it adorns itself to people, so that many people are inclined towards it. Do not be content with this world and do not place your trust in it, for it is not trustworthy. Understand that these worldly temptations will not disappear unless you ignore them."[1]

Shaykh al-Islam Ibn Taymiyyah رحمه الله said, "the Arab poets said:

- The slave is free so long as he is content, and the freeman is a slave so long as he is greedy.

- I followed my desires, and they enslaved me. If only I had been content with my lot, I would be free.

It is said that greed and longing are like chains around the neck and shackles on the feet. Even if the chain is removed from the neck, the feet are still shackled. It was reported that 'Umar b. al-Khaṭṭāb ﷺ said, 'Greed is poverty, and resignation is wealth. When any one of you gives up hope of something, he becomes independent of it.'

This is something which anyone can feel in his heart, for when he gives up hope of something, he no longer wants it or longs for it; he no longer feels in need of it or of the one who can help him to get it. If he longs for and hopes for something, then his heart is attached to it, and he feels that he is in need of it and of the one who he thinks can be the

---

[1] *Tārīkh al-Ṭabarī*, 5/443.

means to this end. This is the case in matters of wealth and power and beautiful images or people, and so forth."[1]

Ibn al-Qayyim رحمه الله said: "The world is a shadow: if you run after it, you will not catch it, but if you turn your back to it, it will follow you."

"All people go to Allah ﷻ after their death, but the happy person is the one who goes to Allah ﷻ while still alive."[2]

[1] Ibn Taymiyyah, *Being a True Slave of Allah* ﷻ.
[2] Sayyid Qutb.

38

In al-Jawzī رحمه الله said: "O my brothers, beware of this *dunyā* [worldly life] for indeed its magic is more dangerous than that of Hārūt and Mārūt: their magic caused separation between a man and his wife, But this *dunyā*'s magic causes separation between the slave and his Lord [Allah جل جلاله]."[1]

"Our five daily prayers are a way to curb over-attachment to anything material. The five prayers regulate our lives with their specific timings to teach us that indeed God is greater than anything else that we might be occupied in at that moment. The dawn prayer teaches us that the most beloved thing to us, comfort, and sleep, should not control us—so we rise up in the cold morning, wash ourselves and pray in an acknowledgement that God is greater than our love of comfort and sleep.

The midday and afternoon prayer teaches us that no matter how engrossed we are with work or the short lunch hour that we so highly value, it's not the purpose of our existence. So we leave it for a few minutes and stand and pray testifying that God is indeed greater. On Friday, we dedicate most, if not all our lunch hour to attend the Friday sermon and prayer.

The dusk prayer, that time when we're finally home and about to spend time with our family, eat dinner or simply relax—we get up and pray together to confirm that God is Greater than any of that. Finally, the night prayer, Isha'—when we're tired after a long day of work and responsibilities ready to fall into bed and sleep, we pray again proving

---

[1] *Al-Mudhish*, p. 386.

that submitting to God is greater than falling into the warm bed. All these serve as constant reminders to us that as much as we love life, we live for a higher purpose."[1]

"Standing in Salah eases you from the backbreaking difficulty of the day. Comfort found in Allah ﷻ at nighttime. When you are relieved of taking insults, working, etc., then come and exhaust yourself in front of Me to regain your strength. And in your Master and your Master alone replenish yourself.

We have to learn to spend more time with Allah ﷻ and enjoy finding comfort with Allah ﷻ and in our conversation with Him; you will find the comfort in Allah ﷻ that you will not find anywhere else. You will find strength in your day because you were with Allah ﷻ in the night, no one to impress or talk to but only Allah ﷻ. Your heart will open when you have that."[2]

[1] Mansoor Ahmed.
[2] Bayyinah TV, Deeper Look, Surah Sharh.

39

Shaykh Ibn 'Uthaymīn رحمه الله said, "A person should not open himself up to worry and regret, because that will upset him and spoil his life and maybe even his religion. That is why the Prophet ﷺ said about a person who has had something he dislikes happen to him even after carrying out all available means, 'Do not say, 'If only I had done this or that, for [saying] 'If only', opens [the door] to the deeds of Satan.'"[1]

If only you knew how much you are worth in the sight of Allah ﷻ you would rip out the sadness from your heart and fill its place with peace.

Those who are frequent in dhikr their worries are little. Sit in the company of a beautiful soul, and you will become infected with their beauty. Whatever challenge you are currently facing, it is no match for Allah ﷻ. Keep your faith. Allah ﷻ will always deliver the best for you.

The greatest lesson you can teach yourself is to be patient. Be patient when you are happy because happiness ends, and be patient when you are sad, because sadness too ends. Nothing is constant. Everything is temporary, except Allah ﷻ. The Eternal, The Everlasting.

[1] *Sharḥ Bulūgh al-Marām*, vol. 11, p. 69.

40

Still not feeling the sweetness of worship? What is going on?[1]

Imam Ibn Taymiyyah رحمه الله identifies one possible reason for such coldness, saying: "If you fail to experience the sweetness of worship and the sense of inner expanse during it, then you must point the finger of blame at your worship. This is because Allah is grateful, meaning that He will certainly reward a person in this world for his actions through peace in the heart, a sense of sweetness and incredible joy. Since these feelings are absent, then it means that the act of worship itself is tarnished by something."[2]

In other words, there is a barrier that is blocking our hearts from tasting the joy of worship, and that barrier is sin.

Try to pinpoint that barrier with brutal honesty:

"Is it in my insincerity?"

"Is it my self-admiration?"

"Is it how I appear in public both online and offline?"

"Is it my fall out with such and such?"

"Is it my finances that's hampering me?"

"Is it envy that's eating me up inside?"

---

[1] Ali Hammuda.
[2] *Madārij al-Sālikīn.*

"Is it my deplorable relationship with my parents?"

"Is it my secret sinful habits?"

"Is it my arrogant feeling that I don't have many sins?"

Wuhayb ibn Ward رحمه الله was asked: "Can a person who [insists on] sins experience the sweetness of worship?" He replied: "No. Not even a person who merely intends to sin."

The same way that an ill body may struggle to enjoy the relish of food, a heart ill with sins will cause a struggle to enjoy the sweetness of worship. Tracing those sins is hard. Tackling them can be even harder. But it is a must, and the good news is that it will only be a matter of time before your soul surrenders to your wishes.

Abū Yazīd al-Bisṭāmī رحمه الله said: "I continued dragging my soul by force to Allah whilst it cried, until it finally surrendered and came with me smiling."

41

"I'll tell you something amazing that I've learned: Our problems are handpicked for us. Never think they are an oversight of God. Our obstacles are given to us to teach us how to climb. That tidal wave you experienced last week—it was sent because you need to learn to swim. The most difficult people and situations in our life are designed by Allah to teach us something or to develop a quality we need to grow."[1]

A wise man once said: "Allah ﷻ never decrees something that is not beneficial for us. Had it not ended you may have gone through so much worse, and nothing is able to stop the decree." Ibn al-Jawzī رَحِمَهُ اللهُ said regarding the divine decree: "The created is a target, and fate is a set of arrows, and the One whom you know [i.e. Allah ﷻ] is the shooter; so what is the way out?"[2]

You should embrace the gifts of Allah ﷻ. Allah ﷻ has so many gifts that He showers upon his slaves which vary. Bigger gifts are through calamities. At the end of every calamity or at its core, there are gifts and goodness that Allah ﷻ has hidden. Only true believers who trust in Allah ﷻ will manage to see beyond the pain and embrace the gift of Allah ﷻ.

In the context of losing partners, Allah ﷻ says: whoever believes in Allah ﷻ, then Allah ﷻ will guide his heart, so the heart can see the blessing which is within the calamity. This is the nature of Allah ﷻ. This is the end of every meeting. You will be rewarded for this hardship.

---

[1] Yasmin Mogahed.
[2] Ibn al-Jawzī, *Seeds of Admonishment and Reform*, pp. 142-143.

Ibn al-Jawzī رحمه الله said: "Truly, most of the blessings I have been given have not been earned by me but rather they are conferred as a result of the planning of The Gentle One alone [Allah عز وجل]."

42

"My brothers, turn down this worldly life [*dunyā*] for it has rejected those who were more enamored by it than you. Take heed from the lessons of those who were before you, before you become a lesson for those who will come after you. This life is intoxicating and enrapturing, and the chants of mankind's nature inherently support it, therefore the lightheadedness of those who drink from it becomes stronger, until the season of profit [to gain good deeds] has passed them by. In Hereafter they wake up from their unconsciousness only to prepare for punishment; the feelings of sorrow overwhelming them, though just the reality of all the good they have missed [of the Hereafter] is a sufficient lash upon them, a fact that they grasp only after death.

Woe to you; death is like the clouds, and gray hair is its raindrops. Whoever reaches the age of seventy would complain of pain even without reason, and so the sensible person is he who wakes up in fear, because he realizes the nearness of death. O you, this life is behind you, and ahead of you is the Hereafter; and to seek what is behind is a retreat and a defeat, whereas victory lies in advancing forward with strong will. The flood of death has arrived so embark for safety onto the ships of righteousness. Woe to you, pay heed and start benefiting yourself from your lifespan, for how long is an earthly creature to live in confusion?

Illnesses distress the bodies necessarily causing emaciation, and you appear as if you were in your grave, lying down on the bed of regret while it is, by Allah ﷻ, harder than a rock. That said, plant [good deeds] during the spring of your life before the onset of sterility afflicts the field that is your body, and amass [good deeds] in your period of capability, setting them aside before the time of weakness and incapability arrives. Prepare your supplies before travelling so you do not suffer poverty during the journey where there is no food to consume. Beware, beware, of [being in a state where you will be among those whom Allah ﷻ said they will say on the Day of Judgment],

> And your soul says, 'Woe is me for having neglected what is due to God and having been one of those who scoffed!' [The Quran 39:56]

The wise and determined is he who acquires his provision [of good deeds] before the time of his return [to his Lord] comes. The root of the tree of strong will and firmness is wise and has perceptive thinking, its branches are seeking advice over problematic issues, and its fruit is taking advantage of available opportunities, and the loss of opportunity in itself is sufficient cause of regret.

I wonder at the one who wastes his lifetime in lazy indifference, until the day the collector of souls [the angel of death] arrives, when he says,

> Indeed, I have repented now. [The Quran, 4:18]

They will say, 'Now we believe in [the truth]', but how can they reach [the truth] from such a distant place? [The Quran, 34:52]"[1]

---

[1] Ibn al-Jawzī, *Seeds of Admonishment and Reform*, pp. 68-70.

43

"Man's need of Him in worshipping Him is greater than man's need of Him in His creating, nourishing, and sustaining man, because worship is man's object and source of fulfilment. There is no correction, no success, no contentment, no delight without worship, and whoever turns away from the remembrance of his Lord,

> But whoever turns away from [guidance] will have a life of great hardship. We shall bring him blind to the Assembly on the Day of Resurrection. [The Quran, 20:124]

> And he will say, 'Lord, why did You bring me here blind? I was sighted before!'

> God will say, 'This is how it is: you ignored Our revelations when they came to you, so today you will be ignored.' [The Quran, 20:126]"[1]

---

[1] Ibn Taymiyyah, *The Relief from Distress*, p. 58.

44

Understanding our journey towards Allah ﷻ

"There are people much greater in number doing things Allah does not want than our gathering here.

> But those who have believed, migrated, and striven for God's cause, it is they who can look forward to God's mercy: God is most forgiving and merciful. [The Quran, 2:218]

Those who migrated and struggled—after belief. What do you get when you do these two? Those people should be hopeful of special mercy and care from Allah ﷻ. Struggle is part of everyone's journey; no one is perfect, sometimes people know about your flaws, sometimes these flaws only hurt you, sometimes they hurt others as well. Every one of us is imperfect in some way and shaytan convinces you to sin based on you not being perfect. Allah ﷻ is saying when you recognize your flaw, and you decide to migrate and move away from it, then you will be the recipient of special love, care, and mercy from Allah ﷻ.

When you start moving away from an object, let's say fire, you move away gradually. In your first step, you would still feel the heat, then in your second step, the heat will still be there but will be much less and will decrease by every coming step until you don't feel it anymore. The presence of the fire is still there, but you have migrated away from it. Imagery of migration is about taking steps, walking towards Allah ﷻ . Even if you fall back a million times, we are hopeful of Allah's ﷻ love and care and we stand up and take a step again, a step away. When you take a step towards Allah[1] ﷻ, Allah ﷻ is taking multiple steps towards you.

Then at the same time struggling. You are struggling against a force against you. It could be a hard test. You must push yourself harder if you want to achieve anything. This life was not made for comfort. Your goal must be worth it for you to be motivated. Athletes are okay with being exhausted, they love it, they don't back down and that is why they achieve their goals and get there. They struggle. Through this you achieve special mercy and care of Allah ﷻ.

Why would someone need forgiveness? When they make a mistake. Allah sees your progress and covered up your past because you migrated and His love and care will shine upon you throughout the process. These people only care about Allah ﷻ seeing their progress and don't care about people appreciating them or not."[2]

A wise man said: "Do not sell your religion for anybody, religion is dearer than your land, family and tribe. When they couldn't live with their religion among their people, they carried their religion and migrated with it."

To be a *ḥanīf*. You must just want the truth and where it leads you. Nothing matters, whether you're kicked out, thrown in the fire, or killed, all that matters is the truth, and nothing else clouds your thoughts. Fearless and unbiased commitment to truth just like Prophet Ibrāhīm ﷺ. When someone genuinely seeks truth, Allah ﷻ guarantees they will arrive where Ibrahim ﷺ arrived without any books or teachers, just like the Companions of the Cave. Allah ﷻ is the protective Friend of those who truly believe. Those who follow

---

[1] See reminder no. 24.
[2] Nouman Ali Khan, An Evening of Reflection.

Him may not have protection of empire, tribe, or family, but Allah ﷻ says those who follow Him have the protection of Allah ﷻ Himself.

45

Al-Ḥasan al-Baṣrī رَحِمَهُ اللهُ said: "Death has exposed this dunyā [worldly life]. It did not leave any happiness in it for the sane."[1]

Why do we fear death? Ibn Ḥazm رَحِمَهُ اللهُ replied: "Because we hate to go from what we have built to what we have destroyed."[2]

Ibn al-Jawzī رَحِمَهُ اللهُ said: "Every breath we take is taking us closer to death. The time we spend in this world is short, the time we are held in our graves long, and the punishment for following our lowly desires calamitous."

---

[1] Aḥmad ibn Ḥanbal, *Al-Zuhd*, p. 316, through the chain of Ibrāhīm b. ʿĪsā al-Yashkurī from al Hasan.
[2] Al Maghrib Institute.

46

Ibn Taymiyyah رَحِمَهُ اللهُ wrote regarding what is to be gained from the good and bad we do: "Good can only be procured by the will of Allah ﷻ, everything He wills, is, and everything He does not will is not. The obstacle to this good on the part of the servant is his sins, anything else that is outside the ability of the servant occurs by the decree of Allah ﷻ. This is so even though the actions of the servant occur by the decree of Allah, exalted is He. Allah ﷻ has appointed the observance of the legislated and the leaving of the prohibited to be the means to pleasure and success.

This is why it is desirable to only attach one's hope to Allah ﷻ and not to fear oppression and wrongdoing from Him, for Allah ﷻ does not oppress the servant in the slightest, instead it is they who oppress themselves. He should, however, fear that Allah ﷻ carry out retribution against him for his sins, and this is why Imam 'Alī رَضِيَ اللهُ عَنْهُ said, The servant should not put his hope in any except his Lord and not fear anything except his sins.

Al-Ḥalīmī رَحِمَهُ اللهُ, said: 'Hope takes on a number of forms:

1) hoping to attain what is desired

2) hoping to keep it after it has been attained

3) hoping to keep at bay all that is disliked and that it does not occur

4) hoping to see the end of anything that is disliked that has already occurred.

When the feeling of hope becomes deeply ingrained in a person, it leads to a state of submissiveness and humility in the same way that this state is achieved when fear takes firm root in the heart. This is because hope and fear go hand in hand, the one who is in a state of fear hopes for the opposite of what he fears—He supplicates to Allah ﷻ and asks of Him; likewise, the one in a state of hope fears losing what he desires and hence takes refuge with Allah ﷻ from this and asks of Him. Hence there is no one who is in a state of fear except that he too is in a state of hope and vice-versa.'"[2]

[1] Al-Ḥalīmī, *al-Minhāj fī Shuʿab al-Īmān.*
[2] Ibn Taymiyyah, *The Relief from Distress*, p. 70.

47

"Observe, my son, the way you deal with the limits of Allah 🕌 and see how you can keep yourself within their bounds. Indeed, he who takes care of these limits is taken care of, and he who doesn't, is left to himself.

There was not a narrating scholar or a preacher where I lived whom I did not sit with, and whenever such a person would arrive from elsewhere, I would go to him. I used to choose of virtuous deeds what suited me, and if I had to choose between two things, I usually chose the right of Allah 🕌. He has planned my life and cultivated me in a beautiful fashion, guiding me towards what is best for me. He has protected me from my enemies, the jealous, and those who might plot against me. He has made everything convenient for my studies of sacred knowledge and sent me books from unexpected places. He gave me good understanding, the ability to memorize and write quickly, and a talent for authoring books.

I lacked nothing of this world. As a matter of fact, things were quite the opposite as Allah 🕌 gave me more than enough. He put a great deal of acceptance of me into peoples' hearts and made the impact of my words leave them not questioning the authenticity of what I had to say. Approximately 200 dhimmīs [People of the Book who live in Muslim lands according to a social contract] have become Muslim at my hands and over 100,000 sinners have repented in my gatherings. More than 20,000 men have announced their repentance from foolish ways during my exhortations.

I used to go around hadith-gatherings of different scholars and run till I was out of breath so no-one would precede me. I would start my day having nothing to eat and finish it having nothing to eat. Never did Allah ﷻ degrade me to take from another person, instead He provided for me in order to protect my honor. The truth is that mentioning all my experiences would take quite a while. And here I am now, and you can see what I have achieved. I will tell you the whole story in one single sentence, and that is Allah's saying:

Fear Allah, and Allah shall teach you. [The Quran, 2:282]

And if you should count the favors of Allah, you could not enumerate them. Indeed, Allah is Forgiving and Merciful. [The Quran, 16:18]"[1]

[1] Ibn al-Jawzī, *Sincere Counsel to the Seekers of True Knowledge*, pp. 43-47.

48

Increasing blessing in your time [1]

Time will shrink, year will feel like a month and a month like a week and a week like a day and a day like an hour. It is on individual and collective levels. You have to realize the value of your time before it is too late, to have blessing in your free time—to do more with less time. More does not always mean more in terms of quantity always. Some people have long lives, but they are fruitless, and others have short lives which are fruitful. Some ways to gain blessing (*barakah* in your time):

- The Prophet ﷺ was a morning person—this time is blessed.

- Avoiding sins and drama: 1) Imam Mālik رَحِمَهُ اللهُ said: I see that Allah ﷻ has put a light in your heart so don't extinguish it with the darkness of sin. Sins take away blessings—they take away the blessings (*barakah*) of wealth, intellect, time and more. All those things are gifts from Him, and He will not allow you to keep them if you don't use them the right way. The light will be extinguished. 2) Not occupying your time with the messiness of sins and their consequences—they take energy, time, gossip, they take your time away.

- Spending time with your family. The Prophet ﷺ said whoever wants to be granted more wealth and extend their life, then let them establish family ties. We think doing more with career and less with family means more wealth—the Prophet ﷺ is saying that in the design of Allah ﷻ spending time with family increases your earnings and blessings (*barakah*) in your time

[1] Lecture by Omar Suleiman.

85

and we trust in Allah ﷻ. It starts with your parents, and so forth. Allah ﷻ will bless your health, Allah ﷻ will put more in your time and guide you to good. Others say Allah ﷻ may increase the remembrance of your name which will allow dua to be made in your name.

- Acts of gratitude, giving your time for others. Your faith will be increased as a result and whatever faculty/blessing you are grateful for, Allah ﷻ will increase that for you. In other words, by using your health to do good, Allah ﷻ will increase your health for you.

- Daily recitation of the Quran, especially Surat al-Baqarah. The Prophet ﷺ said: Recite Surat al-Baqarah, when you do so you are unlocking all sorts of blessings, abandoning it is a form of regret, and it cannot be penetrated or overcome by laziness or sorcery.

- Incorporating remembrance into your routine. Dhikr [remembrance of Allah ﷻ] was always with the Prophet ﷺ— it is part of your life, always, at all times.

- Keep the company of productive people. Seek patience through them. Ibn Abbas ؓ said, "When everyone came back to Madinah who were on journeys he said let's go seek knowledge from them, his friend is narrating and the friend said I'll go play with pigeons." Ibn 'Abbās ؓ went to collect narrations of the Prophet ﷺ— Ibn 'Abbās' house became the first university of Islam.

49

The ability to call upon Allah ﷻ, knowing that He loves to hear me, despite how broken and sinful I am—in that there is a blessing.[1]

A believer reflected saying: "Today I came across an ayah that said '*wa rabbuk*' ['And your Lord']. I see this very often in the Quran, but today for the first time, I felt my heart beat a little harder, as I couldn't help myself but thinking. Not only is this Rabb of ours saying that 'We belong to Him, and to Him shall we return' but He is also saying that He is 'our' Rabb. He is telling us right there...I too love you." Ibn al-Qayyim رحمه الله said, "If the slave truly placed his trust in Allah ﷻ in the truest sense of trust, and all the inhabitants of the heavens and the earth were to plot against him, Allah ﷻ would surely make for him a way out, suffice him, and aid him."[2]

Mufti Menk, may Allah ﷻ reward him, said: "If the Almighty has first place in your life, you won't have to worry about who has the other places. Everything will fall into place and your heart will be content. That's all that matters eventually."[3]

You have 2 choices in life:

1. So remember Me and I will remember you [The Quran, 2:152]

2. They forgot Allah, so He forgot them [The Quran, 9:67]

---

[1] Omar Suleiman, *Allah Loves*.
[2] Ibn al-Qayyim, *Badā'i' al-Fawā'id*, 2/240.
[3] Mufti Menk, Motivational Moments II.

50

The door of Allah ﷻ is always open and the heavens echo with your voice when you call Allah ﷻ invoking Him.

"Allah ﷻ loves to be asked, to be hoped in and desired at times of need, to be supplicated to frequently and resolutely. He can grant all of mankind all their requests without his dominion decreasing in the slightest. Created beings are the exact opposite, they dislike being asked due to their own inability, need and poverty.

Therefore, Wahb bin Munabbih said to one who would frequently appear at the door of the ruler, 'Woe to you! You run to one who would shut his door in your face, display his poverty to you and conceal his riches and you leave One who opens His door to you in the middle of the night and the middle of the day, who displays His richness and proclaims [it]'. Allah ﷻ said: 'invoke Me and I will respond'. Ṭawūs said to 'Aṭā', 'Beware of asking your needs to be met by one who would close his door in your face, instead it is upon you to go to the One whose door is open until the Day of Judgment—One who has ordered you to ask Him and promised you that He would respond.'

Regarding to asking Allah ﷻ Alone for help: this is because man alone cannot promote good for himself or repress harm, hence there is no one who can aid him to promote benefit in his religious and worldly life except Allah ﷻ, Mighty and Magnificent. The servant is in perpetual need of the aid of Allah ﷻ in performing the obligations, leaving the prohibitions, and bearing with patience the variations of the divine decree in this life and after death. The Prophet ﷺ said, 'Be desirous of that which would benefit you and ask the aid of Allah ﷻ and do not become disheartened.'[1][2]

[1] *Muslim*, no. 2664.
[2] Ibn al-Qayyim, *Spiritual Disease and its Cure*.

51

You cannot heal your way to a world where darkness does not exist. It always will. You cannot heal your way into the most physically perfect version of yourself. That is not who you were born for and built to be. You cannot heal your way out of every worry, issue, struggle, grief, sadness, or down day. That is not the point of being alive. The point of healing is not to return to a place where everything is perfect, it is to begin to develop the ability to respond to what is imperfect. You cannot heal your way out of being human, and you were never supposed to.

"Do not carry the worries of this life because this is for Allah ﷻ; do not carry the worries of sustenance because it is from Allah ﷻ; do not carry the anxiety for the future because it is in the Hands of Allah."[1]

Ibn al-Qayyim رحمه الله said: "Whoever is created for Jannah will forever be afflicted with calamities; the believer remains firm and never complains, and the concealment of pain and affliction is one of the attributes of the great. So know full well that you were not denied except to be given, and you were not afflicted except to be cured, nor were you tested except to be purified."[2]

---

[1] Ibn al-Qayyim.
[2] Ibn al-Qayyim, *Al-Fawā'id*, p. 36.

52

"Allah ﷻ lets shaytan speak and shaytan says: not only will I sit and wait for when they come, I will attack from front, behind, right and left:

- **From the front:** Eventually we will stand in front of Allah ﷻ and reach our permanent home. That is a long way into the future. If the Devil is not in your path, you can see your view ahead. He blocks your view and wants you to see something else that is immediate rather than think about what is far down the road [which is better for you]. He wants you to focus on the immediate. What matters is this moment. Now, now, now!—which is the immediate. Humans want the immediate. Shaytan attacks by making us obsessed with the immediate. He pushes you to be impulsive. You tell yourself it is not a big deal and you say just this one time.

- **From behind:** Maybe you used to live a life following the Devil's way and maybe that was fun. You are now walking on the right path, and he says, "Don't you miss those days? Back in the day, do you remember? Good times huh?" He will remind you and say, "Come on; don't you want those days back?" He pulls you into your past. Another way is that he reminds you that you messed up and humiliated yourself, "See you are scum, and you will never be any better"—he will use your past to make you feel hopeless. He sums you up by your past mistakes and he will do this himself and through people as well.

- **From the right:** The implication is that it is from the far right, meaning farther from the right, and you do not see it. Right is good deeds. The Devil himself did good deeds, but he was always a disbeliever, and ungrateful. He will make you do good deeds for the wrong reasons. You will have this appearance of goodness to everyone but all for the wrong reasons, just for showing off and comparison. The terrifying thing about good deeds is that you find the evil of the Devil in Islamic efforts. Islamic workers are the ones he will come after and pit against one another in competition. Sometimes people become impressed with their good deeds, and when you start thinking in this way about your own deeds; you are impressed with yourself, and these are the footsteps of shaytan. Prophet Ibrāhīm ﷺ was building the Ka'bah ,which is the house of Allah ﷻ Himself, yet he was afraid that he was not doing well enough, so that he prayed "O Allah accept it" [The Quran, 2:127]. Humility must come with good deeds. Do not become impressed with your own deeds.

- **From the left:** He makes evil deeds look good. "It's not that bad, just one time, try it. You did hajj, it is just a few sins, you are fine, Ramadan is soon and you will be forgiven anyway, so don't worry." He will even speak on behalf of Allah ﷻ: "Allah ﷻ understands, you are just human. You and Allah ﷻ have a special relationship, He will understand." And even further: "Why is my happiness a bad thing? I want to do what I want to do because it is making me happy." Thus he makes the bad good and the good bad. "I can be good without these things, why do I need prayer to be close to God?" These are shaytan's attacks.

Shaytan concludes as he speaks to Allah ﷻ in the Quran: "You will find that most of them are not grateful." Our real fight against the Devil should be with gratitude.

Sometimes Allah ﷻ makes new opposites that we do not expect: the opposite of "arrogance" is not "humility" in Quran but rather "gratitude". It tells us that when someone is truly grateful, humility comes anyway, and when someone is not grateful, arrogance comes anyway. The four directions are all his attempts to prove you are not grateful. Being grateful is a feeling; Allah ﷻ is telling you that you can counter any of the Devil's attacks, even nullify it, if you can make this feeling of gratitude stronger than any feeling, as it gets rid of your greed, lust, anger and so on.

The Devil is crushing himself by his own feelings. Allah ﷻ is not even crushing him, he is doing it to himself. Allah ﷻ said you are too consumed in your feelings. The Devil wants to make you the same. He makes people such that they create an imaginary sad/negative world where they live. For example, you are traveling, and you couldn't call your mother, and she comes up with an imaginary scenario: you have disowned her, you have disappointed her, something has happened to you, etc. It means you are crushed within yourself. You push yourself into negativity and shaytan wants you to be in negativity. Allah ﷻ says whoever follows that path, I will fill hell with you. The most constant value we should be feeling is gratitude."[1]

---

[1] Nouman Ali Khan, Springfield, Virginia speech.

93

53

"The Quran is there to heal you directly, you don't need someone else, this should overjoy you. Halal and haram are decided by Allah ﷻ. Allah ﷻ has spoken to you directly. Allah ﷻ watches over you before anyone else. Allah watches those who keep on engaging in *taqwā* (being God-conscious) over and over again. Allah ﷻ made it simple to be friends with Him. You need to believe and do good deeds. Faith and *taqwā* is what is needed, and this is something only we can do, no one can do it for us."[1]

> And when he attained manhood, We gave him wisdom and knowledge. Thus We reward the doers of good. [The Quran, 12:22]

> Truly, he who fears Allah and has patience, then surely, Allah does not let the reward of the good-doers be lost. [The Quran, 12:90]

Ibn al-Jawzī says, "Know that the best actions you can store [i.e., add it to your account for the Afterlife] is lowering your gaze from the forbidden, not speaking without need, staying away from punishable deeds, and preferring Him, Glorious is He, over your soul's desires. You are well aware of the hadith of the three who entered the cave and then the rock blocked its entrance. One of them said: 'O Allah, I had my parents and children. I used to stand by my parents with milk and let them drink from it before my kids. If I did that for Your sake, help us now.' One third of the rock moved away. The second one said: 'O Allah, I hired a worker who wasn't pleased with his salary, so I made

---

[1] Nouman Ali Khan.

94

business with it. Then, one day he came to me and said: Will you not fear Allah and give me my salary?' so I said: 'Go to those cows and the people who look after them and take them.' If I did that for Your sake, help us now.' Another third of the rock moved away. The third one said: 'O Allah, I was in love with a cousin of mine but when I approached her, she said: 'Fear Allah and do not break the seal without right,' so I got up, and left her. If I did that for Your sake, help us now.' The whole rock was lifted, and they were able to escape.

Someone dreamt of Sufyān al-Thawrī and he was asked: 'What did Allah do to you [after you died]?' He replied: 'I had only been put into the grave and there I was, in front of the Lord of the Worlds. I entered and straight away met someone who said, 'Sufyān?' I said, 'Yes, I am [Sufyān].' He said, 'Do you remember a day you preferred Allah over your desires?' I said, 'Yes,' [and upon answering] I was immediately served with great plates of food from Paradise."[1]

---

[1] Ibn al-Jawzī, *Sincere Counsel to the Students of Sacred Knowledge*, pp. 74-75.

54

Omar Suleiman, may Allah ﷻ reward him, said: "There is a beautiful saying from Ibn ʿAṭāʾallāh رحمه الله that anytime Allah ﷻ unshackles your tongue to allow it to ask, any time He allows your tongue to move, any time Allah allows you to make a request, know that Allah ﷻ wants to give you something, because He would not have allowed you to make that dua unless He wanted to answer that dua, and the greatest gift of that dua is that Allah ﷻ loves to hear it and you get closer to Him as a result of it. 'When My servants ask you about Me, tell them I am very near. I hear and answer the call of the caller whenever he calls Me,' [The Quran, verse 2:186]. So, when we call upon Allah ﷻ, He is close to us and that is the first gift. The second gift is that He answers our call in a way that befits us, in a way that is in our best interests, in a way that is beneficial to our worldly life and the Hereafter and that does not put us in a more detrimental situation because of our limited scope.

Calling on to Allah ﷻ brings us closer to Him contrary to the perception of people thinking they are too distant to call upon Allah ﷻ. Calling out to Him reduces the gap between us and Him and reduces the distance between us."[1]

"You may not see a way out of your desperate situation, but that doesn't mean the Almighty doesn't have a way. He knows the best time!"[2]

---

[1] Omar Suleiman, *Allah Loves*, pp. 27-29.
[2] Mufti Menk, Motivational Moments.

55

Do not insult. [The Quran, 49:11]

Do not be wasteful. [The Quran, 17:26]

Feed the poor. [The Quran, 22:36]

Do not backbite. [The Quran, 49:12]

Keep your oaths. [The Quran, 5:89]

Do not take bribes. [The Quran, 27:36]

Honor your treaties. [The Quran, 9:4]

Restrain your anger. [The Quran, 3:134]

Do not spread gossip. [The Quran, 24:15]

Think what is good of others. [The Quran, 24:12]

Be good to guests. [The Quran, 51:24-27]

Do not harm believers. [The Quran, 33:58]

Do not be rude to your parents. [The Quran, 17:23]

Turn away from wicked speech. [The Quran, 23:3]

Do not mock others. [The Quran, 49:11]

Walk in a humble manner. [The Quran, 25:63]

Respond to evil with good. [The Quran, 41:34]

Do not say what you do not do. [The Quran, 62:2]

Keep your promises and the trust of others in you. [The Quran, 23:8]

Do not insult others' false gods. [The Quran, 6:108]

Do not deceive people in trade. [The Quran, 6:152]

Do not take properties without right. [The Quran, 3:162]

Do not ask unnecessary questions. [The Quran, 5:101]

Do not be miserly, nor extravagant. [The Quran, 25:67]

Do not call others bad names. [The Quran, 49:11]

Do not claim to be pure [i.e., pious]. [The Quran, 53:32]

Speak nicely, even to the ignorant. [The Quran, 25:63]

Do not ask for repayment of favors and deeds of charity. [The Quran, 76:9]

Make room for others at gatherings. [The Quran, 58:11]

If an enemy wants peace, then accept it. [The Quran, 8:61]

Return a greeting with a better greeting. [The Quran, 4:86]

Do not remind others of the favors you have done to them. [The Quran, 2:264]

56

Provision is from Allah ﷻ

"Pharoah, fearing that a boy from the Children of Israel would grow up and bring an end to his empire, orders his soldiers to kill any baby boy born to the Children of Israel. Moses ﷺ, born at that time, was not only saved, but was taken into the palace of Pharoah and adopted by Pharoah's wife. Refusing any wet nurse that wanted to feed him, he was reunited with his mother, who was hired as a wet nurse for him.

In a time when baby boys were being slaughtered by Pharoah, baby Moses ﷺ was not only saved, but his mother made an income from Pharoah's palace.

Such is the provision of God. It comes from where you do not expect and, at times, from seemingly impossible places. Do your part and trust in Him. What was written for you will never escape you, and, despite their machinations, will come to you even if it is straight from your oppressors' hands."[1]

> There is no moving creature on earth whose provision is not guaranteed by Allah. And He knows where it lives and where it is laid to rest. All is written in a perfect Record. [The Quran, 11:6]

[1] Jinan Yousef

57

Ibn al-Qayyim رحمه الله said, "If the whole of creation were to come together on a single plain and were to call upon Allah ﷻ and seek something from Him, not only does He hear and respond to each and every single one, He knows and hears what is within the hearts of each of them before they say anything. Sometimes, some of them are incapable of putting their request into words, but Allah ﷻ gives them exactly what they wanted without them needing to say anything."

He رحمه الله also said, "Whoever only thinks that his food, his drink, and his health are bounties from Allah ﷻ is unintelligent, for the bounty of Islam, *īmān* [faith], relishing Allah's ﷻ worship, and always turning towards Him are the greatest bounties; however, only those who were granted *tawfīq* [aid and guidance towards success] and the light of intelligence will recognize this."[1]

A wise man said: "When all you have left is your faith, you will realize who got you to where you are; your money and your status in the *dunyā*, as well as your job will not do a single thing for you if you died today, when you need something you will go to Allah ﷻ running. All the while you forget Him when it comes to what He has given you now. Your wealth, your children, your parents—everything you have is because of Allah ﷻ. He is the Most Merciful and He is the only one worth praising, He who looks after us even though we are ungrateful. Remember how you reached where you are now."

---

[1] *Madārij al-Sālikīn*, vol. 1, p. 277.

58

"Imam al-Shāṭibī رَحِمَهُ ٱللَّٰه, who was blind, composed poems and writings worth hundreds of pages. In his poem he says you have to know that the rope of God amongst us is the Quran. It is called a rope because it is something you hold on to in a time of need to reach a goal. For us the Prophet ﷺ said that the Quran is the rope of Allah ﷻ extending from the heavens.

You only struggle and don't have time when you don't want to have the time or don't want to struggle. To have a relationship with this book [i.e., the Quran], you have to struggle against yourself. There will be opposition, the book won't come easy to you. Give five minutes to the Quran a day. Come back after a month and reflect among the unlimited doors that will open for you. There is no better way to get close to Allah ﷻ except with His word. When someone came to ʿUthmān ؓ asking how to get close to Allah ﷻ, he replied, 'I don't know an easier way than with His words.'"[1]

"The basis of Islam is moral good, but it must be followed by the religious good. But then what about people who think that because they are already morally good, they don't need to be religiously good, who usually say 'I am a good person, I don't do harm to others,' or 'I don't need to pray five times to be a good person'? When people don't do the religious good and only do the moral good, this means that they think Allah's ﷻ standard is lower than theirs which is a scary place to be."[2]

[1] Suhaib Webb.
[2] Nouman Ali Khan.

59

Ibn Taymiyyah رحمه الله said: "I do not look to anyone but Him with love and fear and hope; for the eye looks towards that to which the heart is attached. Whoever loves a thing, or has hope in it or fears it, will turn towards it. If there is no love for it in the heart, or hope or fear or hatred, or any other emotion that ties the heart to it then the heart will not turn deliberately towards it or look towards it. If it accidentally glances at it, it will be like a man who happens to glance at a wall or anything else that means nothing to him.

So, he hears with the Truth, sees with the Truth, strikes with the Truth, and walks with the Truth. He loves that which Allah ﷻ loves and hates that which Allah ﷻ hates; he takes as friends those whom Allah ﷻ takes as friends and regards as enemies those whom Allah ﷻ regards as enemies, He fears Allah ﷻ with regard to His creation, but he does not fear created beings with regard to his duties towards Allah ﷻ. He places his hope in Allah ﷻ with regard to His creation, but he does not place his hope in created beings with regard to his duties towards Allah ﷻ. This is the sound, believing Muslim heart. Which has perfect faith in Allah ﷻ alone and truly understands the message of the Prophets and Messengers."[1]

He رحمه الله also said: "Abū Ṭālib [The uncle of the Prophet ﷺ] knew full well that Muhammad was the Messenger Allah ﷺ, he also loved him—but his love of him did not arise as a result of his love of Allah ﷻ, rather due to relations—this is why when he was asked to articulate the Testimony of Faith on his death bed, he did not accept to do so—because he loved his [pagan] religion more than he loved his cousin.

---

[1] Ibn Taymiyyah, *Al-'Ubūdiyyah*.

Now, were he to have loved him because he was the Messenger of Allah ﷺ, for sure he would have said it then."[1]

[1] Ibn Taymiyyah, *The Relief from Distress.*

60

Ibn Taymiyyah رحمه الله said, "The slave [of Allah ﷻ] should know that wisdom and justice lies in what was decreed for him, not in what he thinks should have happened."[1]

A wise man said, "Congratulations to those who leave the world before it deserts them, to those who build their graves before they enter them; and to those who please their Lord before they meet Him."

---

[1] Ibn Taymiyyah, *The Relief from Distress.*

61

Trials [1]

From an Islamic perspective, tribulations are not meant to oppress individuals. Instead, their aim is to enable people to realize the truth about their existence and their potential for spiritual growth. Although they may appear bad on the surface, tribulations are, in reality, good and beneficial. Out of His mercy ﷻ, Allah ﷻ ordains only goodness for human beings.

As part of Allah's ﷻ wisdom, Allah ﷻ tests individuals with trials and tribulations that are tailored to match their specific needs, weaknesses, circumstances and abilities. This is to provide as much benefit as possible and to facilitate the spiritual and personal growth that they require. Although we may not always be aware of them, the meaning and values are inherent in these trials. Often, they are recognized later during insightful moments of retrospection.

Everything on Earth is part of the Divine test that Allah ﷻ has put forth for humans. Hardship and ease, wealth and poverty, good and bad; all are intended to be tests. During times of both ease and blessings, we are expected to be grateful. During times of difficulty and hardship, we should be patient. In accordance with Allah's mercy ﷻ, Allah ﷻ would never test humans with tribulations that are beyond their capacity to bear. Allah ﷻ reassures us:

[1] Aid al Qarni, *Don't Be Sad.*

Allah does not charge a soul except [with that which is within] its capacity. It will have [the consequence of] what [good] it has gained, and it will bear [the consequence of] what [evil] it has earned. [The Quran, 2:286]

The above verse indicates that every trial you face in your lifetime is within your ability to cope with and manage. No matter how difficult the trial is, it will never exceed your capacity to endure and overcome it. This is a promise from Allah ﷻ, and Allah ﷻ never fails in His promises.

But you prefer the life of this world. Although the Hereafter is better and more lasting. [The Quran, 87:16-17]

The highest degree of comfort and pleasure in this life is not free from hardships and grief. Secondly, this world is not permanent. We experience it in our daily life when a king of today becomes a pauper tomorrow. A vigorous youth of today becomes senile tomorrow. Whereas the Hereafter is free of these defects. All its comforts and blessings are much better and cannot be compared to that of this world.

Consider this scenario: it is said to a person that there are two houses, one of which is a magnificent mansion, the other an ordinary, substandard house. He has a choice to take the mansion but only for a month or two afterward, but he will have to vacate the mansion, or he may take the ordinary house which he will permanently own. Which of the two houses would a wise person prefer? Obviously, the second house. On this analogy, one should prefer the blessings of the Hereafter which in this case are not only everlasting but far more superior to the worldly comforts which are only temporary. Only an unfortunate fool will prefer the blessings of this life compared to the Hereafter.

A man was once thrown into the cage of a lion from which Allah ﷻ saved him from its claws. He was later asked, 'What were you thinking about at the time?' He said, 'I was considering the saliva of a lion—whether it is considered by scholars to be pure or impure.' [Meaning 'Whether, when I die, I will be in a state of purity or not after having been touched by its saliva.'] The pious people of the past had no interest in this world. In fact, they used this world to get the best of the Hereafter. Whatever situation they were in they would always link it back to Allah's ﷻ religion.

The Messenger of Allah ﷺ said: "If this world is worth the wing of a mosquito to Allah ﷻ, Allah ﷻ would not have given the disbelievers [even] a drink of water."[1]

This world is not even worth the wing of a mosquito! If this is the worth of this world, why are we so attached to it?

---

[1] Sunan Ibn Mājah, no. 4110.

62

In moments of sadness, shaytan comes and wants you to let go of Allah ﷻ. Faith in Allah ﷻ does not take difficulty or sadness away but it makes us strong enough to go through them without breaking. Your connection with Allah ﷻ is that of intimate and close friendship. You speak with Him every day. It is a daily interaction which is strong, and it affects our emotions and the way we think. For some of us Allah ﷻ becomes a distant concept. It should be deep and intimate. The benefit of the five prayers: intimate conversation.

Life was designed with difficulties included. Just because we are believers, it does not mean our problems will disappear. Picture that Allah ﷻ created us in a storm at sea and we are worried about sinking—faith gives us strength and the ability to navigate and pass through the storm.

Two of the hardest burdens in this life are sadness (such as for the past; feeling sad is not a sign of not having faith—Prophet Yaʿqūb ﷺ grieved for Yūsuf, and our Prophet ﷺ for Khadījah, when she passed away May Allah ﷻ be pleased with her) and fear (such as worrying about the future). Yet again when the mother of Mūsā ﷺ was told to throw her child in the water (where he may have sunk), Allah ﷻ told her not to be sad or afraid. Allah ﷻ helps you navigate these feelings and allows you to stay safe and sane through them. You and I are not capable of controlling our emotions without Allah ﷻ. Strength is given by Allah ﷻ to go through these emotions.

"Rabb" is the one who keeps making this easy and gives you constantly more than you deserve. He makes sure you always grow out of weakness and sadness. He is the One who makes sure you do not fall apart or stay in the same difficult place. He is in charge of what you do. The power that the creation has over you bounces off and goes away. Reality does not change but you change, as you keep struggling to straighten yourself.

63

Feel something with the Quran

A wise man said, "We have to feel humility and respect towards the word of Allah ﷻ. This will make you feel in awe of it. These are words from Allah ﷻ. We have to be grateful to Allah ﷻ for sending us this timeless revelation that is so full of love and care, meant to help us and support us. Allah ﷻ says 'I will respond to you if you respond to Me.' We have to make an attempt to understand the Quran and respond by understanding it and putting it into practice. Dua is our reply, but He wants us to respond to His call—it is a two-way relationship, a conversation.

We have to be overwhelmed with joy in having it—no treasure can be compared with it. Allah ﷻ asks why your heart has not moved. Is reading the Quran just part of our culture now, something you do like the other thing you do—not something that moves your heart—so that your heart does not feel anything and becomes hard to it? Allah ﷻ says people are distracted—the worldly life distracts people. If we allow our hearts to stay hard, the majority becomes corrupt and become shaytan's playing field.

Allah ﷻ tells you that it is not hopeless if you feel that your heart is dead—Allah ﷻ brings the dead earth back to life. But how is the earth brought back to life? When there is no water, the earth dies. Allah's ﷻ pure words come from the heavens, just like rain. Allah ﷻ is telling us: think about connecting to and responding to Him. The Word of Allah ﷻ has to be taken in over again and over again because it always cleans something in you. Allah ﷻ talks to you, allow that conversation to grow—so that you can be grateful.

Have you thought about the Quran, 'I need this book in the same way I need my basic needs?' If you have not felt gratitude for the Quran, you have lost sight of what you are doing. Be grateful because it has made your life better."

64

Every human is a slave. You are either a slave of your desires or a slave of Allah ﷻ. You either live life by your own rules or the rules of Allah ﷻ. How can the heart travel to God if it is chained by its desires?

Ibn al-Qayyim رحمه الله said: "O son of Adam! Sell this world for the Hereafter and you will win both, sell the Hereafter for this world and you will lose both." Islam is not a buffet where you pick and choose what suits you. Do not obey your desires, obey Allah ﷻ. Ibn Taymiyyah رحمه الله said: "Imprisoned is he, whose heart is imprisoned away from Allāh. Captured is he, who is captured by his desires."

Al-Fuḍayl b. ʿIyāḍ رحمه الله was asked "What do you find the strangest of all things?" He said: "The heart that knows Allah ﷻ, yet still disobeys Him. You were born and will die alone; you will go to the grave alone and be questioned alone on Judgment Day."

> Close friends, on that Day, will be enemies to each other, except for the righteous and God fearing... [The Quran, 43:67]

We prepare for uncertain matters in our lives like marriage, but do we prepare for the one event that is definitely going to happen—death? At fajr you are asleep, at ẓuhr you are busy, at ʿaṣr you are tired, at maghrib you are watching television, at ʿishāʾ you are eating. You can dodge prayer, but not death. The first thing a slave will be held to account for is *ṣalāh*. If we fall short on that, then we will fall short on what is to come. Do not fear missing sleep, fear a day on which there will be no sleep. Expecting Paradise whilst neglecting prayer is like waiting for a train to arrive at the airport.

Nouman Ali Khan says: "When salah is in place then you can ask Allah ﷻ for things. The most important thing is to ask Allah ﷻ for forgiveness. The people of salah are the ones who can ask Allah ﷻ for forgiveness. Forgiveness is the key to everything, but prayer is the key to forgiveness."

Everyone dreams to be in Jannah, but Allah ﷻ says: "[Paradise is not obtained] by your wishful thinking." [paraphrased from The Quran, 4:123]

The Prophet ﷺ said: "The world is a prison for the believer and a Paradise for the unbeliever"[1]. Your release here, sooner or later, will be coming to an end. Ibn al-Qayyim رحمه الله said: "If you could hear the sound of the pens of the angels writing your name among those who remember Allah ﷻ, you would die out of joy."

Ibn Al-Qayyim رحمه الله said: "He whom Allah ﷻ has predestined to enter Paradise, the reasons which will cause his entrance shall spring from calamities; he whom Allah ﷻ has predestined to enter the Hellfire, the reasons which will cause his entrance shall spring from lusts."

'Umar b. al-Khaṭṭāb ؓ said "Get used to a rough life, for luxury does not last forever." Do not be overly pleased by easy times. Verily, gold is tested for its purity by fire. Likewise, a righteous servant is tested by tribulations. Run back to your Lord, for His mercy overcomes His wrath. How long will the person be happy with his worldly life knowing that his ultimate home is the grave? Every single limb and organ in your body will speak up and bear witness against every action you committed in this *dunyā*. "Not a word is said except that there is

[1] Al-Tirmidhī, no. 2324.

a watcher by him ready to record it." [The Quran, 50:18]. This, of course, includes all that we post online.

Ibn Taymiyyah رحمه الله said: "Make *tawbah* [sincere repentance] not just for sins that you have committed, but also for obligations you have not fulfilled." I pray that the comfort of our graves exceeds the comfort of our beds.

65

Ibn al-Jawzī ﷽ said: "Take heed, my son, for your own benefit, and regret your previous shortcomings. Work hard to attain company of those who have achieved perfection while you still have time. Water your tree while there is still some moisture left in it and remember the time you have wasted, for that indeed is a sufficient reminder. As time has passed, the delight of laziness has vanished, and the levels of virtuous deeds have been missed. Indeed, our pious predecessors loved to enact every virtue and would cry out for missing just one.

Know, my son, that days consist of hours and hours are made of the breaths you take. Every breath is a treasure chest, so beware of letting a breath pass by without benefit. You do not want to find an empty treasure chest on the Day of Judgment and be filled with regret. Indeed, a man once said to 'Āmir b. 'Abdi Qays: 'Stop, I want to talk to you,' so he said to him, 'Hold the sun in your hands [i.e., stop time] so I can talk to you.'"[1]

"How excellent are the people who have abandoned sweet dreams, withdrawing from that for which they erected their feet [night prayers]. Standing up to fatigue themselves in the dark, seeking a portion of the divine blessing. When the night comes, they stay up, and when the day arrives, they derive lessons from it. When they look at their faults they seek forgiveness, and when they think about their sins they cry and feel dejected. O dwellings of the beloved, where are your inhabitants? O places of sincerity, where are your residents? O spots of the pious, where are your people? O places of nightly prayer, where are your visitors? I have, by Allah, traveled around and found

---

[1] Ibn al-Jawzī, *Sincere Counsel to the Seekers of Sacred Knowledge*, pp. 48-49.

these people extinct. Those who used to stay awake at night have gone away and the lovers of sleep are left. These times have sought eating of lusts to replace fasting."[1]

"When a person looks at the time spent in this world, let us say sixty years, he can see that thirty of it is spent sleeping, fifteen or so is spent in childhood and most of what's left goes to chasing after desires, food, and wealth. When he accounts for what is left, he finds that much of it is nothing but showing off and heedlessness. The price of eternal life is the hours of his life, but what is left of them for him to buy it with?

> And race like racehorses and be the first,
> for they are loaned to you, and you shall return them."[2]

[1] Ibid, p .51.
[2] Ibid.

66

"Eating is easy, being healthy is hard; being lazy is easy, exercising is hard; not studying is easy, studying is hard. But every time you stick with the easy, it is followed by long-term difficulty. Allah ﷻ wants long-term ease for you. The laws of Allah ﷻ are not hard. You think they are, and the thinking comes from the thought that these short-term-ease choices have no consequences.

Allah ﷻ does not want hardship for you in the long-term. He will put you through short-term difficulty for long-term ease. Ramadan is a short-term difficulty for a whole life of God-consciousness [*taqwā*]."[1]

It will make you so aware of Allah ﷻ that you will avoid drinking or eating at times after Ramadan when you reach to eat or drink. Allah ﷻ wants that for you because He cares for you and wants to facilitate your path to Him, to Paradise.

> It was in the month of Ramadan that the Quran was revealed as guidance for mankind, clear messages giving guidance and distinguishing between right and wrong. So, any one of you who is present that month should fast, and anyone who is ill or on a journey should make up for the lost days by fasting on other days later. God wants ease for you, not hardship. He wants you to complete the prescribed period and to glorify Him for having guided you, so that you may be thankful [The Quran, 2:185]

"Your body doesn't even bother to produce the hunger hormones at lunchtime anymore because your mind has made a firm, disciplined,

[1] Nouman Ali Khan.

principled, pre-planned decision to postpone the meal. Sure, the body tries for the first few days but when it sees that there's no point, it gives up. Mind over matter. This invites the question: If I can do this for the most basic primal urges, what else can I harness this discipline for? If I put my mind to something, I can change the chemicals in my body. No meaningful growth has ever come without calculated restraint, and Ramadan develops this invaluable skill within you. The question is: Where will you apply it?"[1]

---

[1] Shaykh Abdelrahman Badawy.

67

One of the scholars said, "I have a need for Allah ﷻ, so I invoke Him and He grants me the delight of knowing Him and the sweetness of discoursing with Him, which makes me desire that my need not be swiftly answered for fear that my soul become distracted from this, because the soul only desires what it wants and when it attains this it turns away."

Ibn al-Mubārak said, "Umar b. 'Abd al-Raḥmān b. Mahdī informed me that he heard Wahb bin Munabbih saying, 'A sage said: I am embarrassed before Allah ﷻ that I worship Him for desire of the reward of Paradise [i.e., only for this] so that I end being like a bad laborer, I only work if I am paid. I am embarrassed before Allah ﷻ that I worship Him for fear of Hell [i.e., only for this] so that I end up being like a bad servant, I only work when threatened. However, the love I have for Him causes me to do such deeds that no other love does."[1]

---

[1] Recorded by Abū Nuʿaym, *al-Ḥilyah*, 4/53-54.

68

Whatever you have will end, but whatever Allah ﷻ has is everlasting

We associate different brands with different qualities. That brand is inexpensive; this one is reliable, that one is trendy, this one is high quality. Imagine if we were to stamp everything in this world with an expiration date. Our parents, our children, our spouses, our jobs, our computers, our cars. Temporary—that is the brand of this life by default. Because it is ours, because it is of this world, it takes the quality of the brand: ending, temporary.

What is with Allah ﷻ is nothing like the cheap brand of this world. What is with Allah ﷻ is something else altogether—it is everlasting. How beautiful that Allah ﷻ calls good deeds *"al-bāqiyāt"*—the everlasting ones. The only thing in this life that does not take on the cheap, temporary quality of the brand of this *dunyā* is our good deeds.

> Whatever you have will end, but whatever Allah has is everlasting. And We will certainly reward the steadfast according to the best of their deeds. [The Quran, 16:96]

> Wealth and children are the adornment of this worldly life, but the everlasting good deeds are far better with your Lord in reward and in hope. [The Quran, 18:46]

Five lamps and five dark matters [1]

---

[1] Abū Bakr al-Ṣiddīq ﷺ.

There are five dark matters and five lamps:

1. Love of this world is darkness, and the fear of Allah ﷻ is its lamp.

2. Sin is darkness, and its lamp is repentance.

3. The grave is darkness, and its lamp is 'None has the right to be worshipped but Allah, and Muhammad is the Messenger of Allah'.

4. The Hereafter is darkness, and its lamp is the good deed.

5. The *sirāṭ* is darkness, and its lamp is certainty of faith.

69

The Mouse and The Camel

"A mouse once went to the market and met a great ferocious camel. The mouse fell in love with the camel from the first sight. She then pulled the camel's nose-string, smiled, and waved to him asking him to follow her to her home. When they reached her home and stood by its entrance, she realized that there was no way the camel could enter her tiny house. The camel then said to the mouse: "You either get a house that befits your loved one or fall in love with one that befits your house".

Ibn al-Qayyim ﷦ narrated this ancient tale in one of his books[1] and commented: "You either offer a prayer [*ṣalāh*] in a quality that befits the Majesty and Magnificence of your Lord, or you go find yourself another Lord [not just idols but rather desires, money, and worldly affairs being prioritized] that befits the quality of your prayer".

If you get yourself into the habit of delaying your *ṣalāh* and failing to offer it in good quality, then you should be mentally and emotionally prepared for much failure and disappointment in every aspect of your life. Do you not realize that success has been closely associated with *ṣalāh* from the beginning of Islam? Hence in the call to prayer, the call says, "Come to Salah. Come to success."

Al-Ḥasan al-Baṣrī ﷦ said: "If you view your prayer [*ṣalāh*] as something inconsequential and allow it to be subject to compromise,

---

[1] Ibn al-Qayyim, *Badā'i' al-Fawā'id*.

then what would be the one thing you cling to and see as critically important for your salvation?"[1]

123

70

I wonder how Muʿādh ibn Jabal ﷺ felt when he heard the Messenger of Allah ﷺ saying, "O Muʿadh, by Allah, I most certainly love you."

And how did ʿAbdullāh ibn ʿAbbās ﷺ feel when the Messenger of Allah ﷺ embraced him and said, "O Allah teach him the Book."

Or what ʿAlī ibn Abī Ṭālib ﷺ felt when he heard the Messenger of Allah ﷺ saying, "Tomorrow, I will definitely hand the banner to a man who loves Allah and His Messenger ﷺ, and whom Allah and His Messenger ﷺ love also," and then he found out that he was the one?

And how did ʿUthmān ibn ʿAffān ﷺ feel when he fully supplied the army heading to Tabuk, and the Messenger of Allah ﷺ said, "Nothing ʿUthman does after today could ever harm him"?

Or how Abū Mūsā al-Ashʿarī ﷺ felt when the Messenger of Allah ﷺ said, "If you could have only seen me while I was listening to your recitation yesterday."

And how did Al-Sāʾib ibn Yazīd ﷺ feel when only the patch of hair that the Messenger of Allah ﷺ wiped on his head remained black, when the remainder of his hair turned gray with old age?

And what emotions did the Anṣār experience when the Messenger of Allah ﷺ said to them, "If all people were to go one way, and the Ansar were to take another, I would choose the path of the Anṣār." [An Arab expression meaning that the addressed is even more beloved than one's own parents.]

And how did the Anṣār feel when the Prophet of Allah ﷺ spoke about them saying, "The sign of belief is love for the Anṣār, and the sign of hypocrisy is feeling animosity toward them."

And what were the feelings of Al-Ṣiddīq ﷺ when the Messenger of Allah ﷺ said, "If I were to take a bosom friend, I would have taken Abū Bakr as my bosom friend."

How did Aisha [may Allah ﷺ be pleased with her] feel when the Messenger of Allah ﷺ replied unhesitatingly with her name when asked who was the most beloved person to him?

And what were the feelings of Bilāl ibn Rabāḥ ﷺ when Allah's Messenger ﷺ said to him, " O Bilāl, tell me about the deed in which you place most hope, for I have heard the sound of your shoes striking the ground in front of me in Paradise."

And how did 'Umar ibn al-Khaṭṭāb ﷺ feel when he sought permission to enter upon the Messenger of Allah, and he ﷺ told the doorman, "Allow him to enter and give him glad tidings of Paradise."

How did all the Sahabah feel while seeing the Messenger ﷺ morning and evening?

And how are we going to feel when we see in the *ākhirah* [the Hereafter] the Messenger of Allah ﷺ, and he says to us, "You are my brothers for whom I have cried in my anticipation to meet; you are my brothers who have believed in me without ever seeing me."

Oh Allah make us among them. *O Allah send Your peace and blessings on Muhammad and the family of Muhammad.*

71

"You did not find that post for nothing. Allah ﷻ allowed you to see it for a reason. There are millions of blog posts out there, but you are reading this one right now. I just want you to know that Allah ﷻ is right there with you and He loves you more than you will ever understand. He knows what you are going through. He knows what you want. He knows what you need. He will not let you down, so just rely on Him and trust Him. Everything is going to be okay; you just have to let His plan work out. If you are looking for a sign or something to give you some hope and strength, then let this be it. Don't give up!"[1]

Allah ﷻ sends us signs in various ways. Sometimes we are in the midst of an evil thought or about to act upon one when suddenly a friend calls us, or our mothers call us whether in person or on the phone; we suddenly see a Quranic post; suddenly a verse is being recited; suddenly you are prevented from that action. This, my beloved brothers and sisters, is no coincidence. This is from your loving and caring Master, Allah ﷻ. He wants you to go to Jannah. Yes, He wants you to go to Jannah and everything He does for us is with that in mind. Read that again.

> We shall show them Our signs in every region of the earth and in themselves, until it becomes clear to them that this is the Truth. Is it not enough that your Lord witnesses everything? [The Quran, 41:53]

[1] Mobeen Hakim.

72

"Abandon grave and minor sins, for this is the essence of fearing Allah ﷻ. Do as a man walking in a road full of thorns who avoids what he sees. Do not make little of a minor sin. Mountains are made of pebbles.

The Prophet's ﷺ saying "Fear Allah wherever you are" means that one should fear Allah ﷻ in secret and public, whether people see him or not. When a person knows that Allah ﷻ sees him wherever he is and that he knows all about his affairs whether secret or public, he will abandon evil deeds committed in secret.

God is always watching over you. [The Quran, 4:1]

Wuhayb bin al-Ward said, "Fear Allah ﷻ in the very same degree He has power over you and be shy before Him in the very same degree He is near you." A man said to him, "Advise me." Wuhaib said, "Fear Allah ﷻ and do not consider Him the least one Who looks at you. Once a man tried to seduce a Bedouin woman. When they were alone, he said, 'None sees us but the planets.' She said, 'Where is the Being Who created them?'"

Imam Aḥmad رحمه الله used to say, "If you are alone one day, do not say 'I am alone', but say 'There is an All-Watcher with me.' Never think that Allah ﷻ is unaware even for an hour or that hidden things are not known by Him."

"When the Prophet ﷺ advised Muʿādh to fear Allah ﷻ in secret and public, he guided him to the means that might help him in this regard. He advised Muʿādh to be humble before Allah ﷻ as he would be humble before a widely respected man in his family. This means that he should always feel that Allah ﷻ is near him and that He knows the ins and outs of him. Once he has such feeling in his heart, he will fear Allah ﷻ." [1]

[1] Ibn Rajab al-Ḥanbalī, *Jāmiʿ al-ʿUlūm wa-l-Ḥikam*, pp. 224-226.

73

"O you whose eyes in this life are tearless, tomorrow on the Day of Judgment the sun will be brought close to your head upon which the mouths of your veins will open so that each hair in your body will cry on its own. The sky will look as if it is violently dusting off its sleeves because of the maelstrom of cataclysms, the stars shall be scattered apart, and then the horror of The Day arrives to rip apart the fabric of the universe.

The blowing of winds in this life might shake trees, but the blowing of the horn shall shake everything in existence; one blow shall bring forth death, while the next blow shall revive. Let this not surprise you; do you not see this scene reflected in the present life, when the blast of winter cold causes trees to become as if lidless effigies of themselves, followed by the puffs of spring that bring back the spirit of life to these dormant trees?"[1]

Ask yourself, are you preparing for such a day or have you turned away from The Most Merciful?

"O you who turned away from his Lord, what else kept you away from your Lord and you turned to instead? Why have you let yourself be led by another? [It is time] for you to stand on the right path.

Therefore, no one [should] ever object when He comes in Grace saying to His slaves: 'Is there anyone who requests anything so I fulfil it for him?'

---

[1] Ibn al-Jawzī, *Seeds of Admonishment and Reform*, p. 175.

I wonder at you! Allah draws near to you though He is in no need for you, whereas you are arrogant with Him though you are in need of Him. When you are far, He draws you near to Him and when you are negligent, He reminds you. He did not favor any other creation over you but nevertheless you still favor everything over Him. Lower the head of your regret before the commencement of the Day at which you are blamed because then you will not have the face to answer any of that."[1]

[1] Ibid., pp. 134-138.

74

I learned the meaning of love the day I started to pray. I realized love means to show up, every day, every time. No matter what, no matter how you feel, love is just *being there*. Love is being committed. No matter how you feel—confused, tired, depressed, exhausted—never abandon ṣalāh, never abandon Allah ﷻ. It is the strongest sign of faith when you love Allah ﷻ so much that you only see the world around you in light of that love.

You love anything if it is pleasing to Allah ﷻ and you dislike anything if it displeases Allah ﷻ. When you love Allah ﷻ this much, you will love people based on how much obedience they show to Allah ﷻ and how hard they are striving. Of the qualities Allah ﷻ wants of a person is God-consciousness (*taqwā*). The Quran wants us to change for the better. The purpose of these teachings is for us to become people who are grateful and thoughtful, people of *taqwā*. The only true way to protect ourselves from disappointing Allah ﷻ is to seek the protection of Allah ﷻ.

Nouman Ali Khan expanded on this and said, "Allah ﷻ is saying those of you who have taken steps to believe, be mindful from disappointing Allah ﷻ, protect yourselves from distancing yourself from Allah ﷻ because everything we do either brings us closer to Allah ﷻ or farther. Allah ﷻ wants us being protective of anything that will take us away from Him.

Taqwā is an emotional state, a state of the mind. *Taqwā* is being aware of Allah's ﷻ presence. How do we maintain it? By surrounding ourselves with the kind of company that keeps this alive for us. There is company that makes us forget Allah ﷻ. They are almost agitated at anything that reminds them of Allah ﷻ and it either is annoying or turns into a joke. When you go through that over and over again, you condition yourself not to bring Allah ﷻ up when in certain company and you allow that to happen. Be mindful of the things you become accustomed to. This is about protecting ourselves. Those of you who believe, protect yourself from becoming one that acts in a way where Allah's ﷻ presence is not recognized. Or that He is loving, watching, the One giving gifts, etc.

Protect yourself in a way that shows you are doing justice to Allah ﷻ . Be mindful from distancing yourself, the way He deserves it. How can we do this? Allah ﷻ is saying when you do as much as you can then you are somewhat doing justice. There is a difference between what I can and what I am comfortable with. You have to experience discomfort and go out of this comfort zone to experience *taqwā*. If today is my last day, what should I be doing? You are heading to Allah ﷻ, not your things. It becomes easier to move out of the comfort zone. The previous nations lost *taqwā* and as a result all that happened."

75

In this world you will never truly be happy no matter what Allah ﷻ gives you. This place is designed to break your heart.

How could you feel worthless? You are not the servant of al-Lāt, or al-'Uzzā, or fashion, you are the slave of Allah ﷻ. Allah ﷻ has chosen you among billions and has blessed you with Islam. Pain and suffering only become negative when it creates a barrier between you and Allah ﷻ. Pain becomes a positive motivation for you when it brings you back to Allah ﷻ. 'O my slaves come back to your Lord', this is a reminder that Allah ﷻ wants you to come back to Him. He wants you to return to Him because He wants the best for you.

Do not get stressed out over things that have not happened. Everything has been decreed already. If you have Allah ﷻ you have everything you desire, if you do not have Allah ﷻ, you have nothing, and everything you attain will bring you misery.

Ibn al-Qayyim رحمه الله mentioned, "Worries, distress and grief are indeed caused by two factors:

1. Desiring the life of this world and having eagerness for it.

2. Falling short in [performing] acts of piety and obedience [to Allah ﷻ].

76

Abū Dharr quoted God's Messenger ﷺ as saying that, among the things he transmitted from Allah ﷻ was that He has said, "My servants, I have made oppression unlawful for myself and I have made it unlawful among you, so do not oppress one another. My servants, you are all straying except those whom I guide, but if you ask for my guidance, I will guide you. My servants, you are all hungry except those whom I feed, but if you ask me for food, I will feed you. My servants, you are all naked except those whom I have clothed, but if you ask me for clothing, I will clothe you.

My servants, you are all sinning night and day, but I forgive all sins, so if you ask me for forgiveness, I will forgive you. My servants, you will not be able to injure me and succeed in such a purpose, neither will you be able to benefit me and succeed in such a purpose. My servants, even if the first and last of you, men, and jinn, were as pious as the one with the most pious heart among you, that would not cause any increase in my dominion.

My servants, if the first and last of you, men, and jinn, were as wicked as the man with the most wicked heart among you, that would not cause any diminution in my dominion. My servants, if the first and last of you, men, and jinn, were to stand in one plain and make requests of me and I were to give every man what he asked, that would make no more diminution of what I possess than a needle would when put into the sea. My servants, they are only your deeds which I put to your account and then pay you in full for them; so, let him who experiences good praise God, and let him whose experience is different blame no one but himself."[1]

Prophet Ibrāhīm ﷺ said, "Those idols you have worshipped, you and your forefathers, are my enemies; not so the Lord of the Worlds, Who created me. It is He who guides me; He who gives me food and drink; He who cures me when I am ill; He who will make me die and then give me life again; And He who will, I hope, forgive my faults on the Day of Judgement." [The Quran, 26:75-82]

Prophet Ibrāhīm ﷺ knows Allah ﷻ will feed him and will help him. Everything we have, have ever had, is from Allah ﷻ. Even the home we grew up in; on the outside yes, our parents gave us a home but in reality, it is Allah ﷻ. Being able to benefit from the food you eat, the food being able to go down your throat is Allah ﷻ. He had this level of trust in Allah ﷻ at the worst time of his life. There is a calmness that comes from letting go. From letting Allah ﷻ take over.

[1] *Mishkāt al-Maṣābīḥ*, no. 2326.

135

77

Ibn Taymiyyah's advice رَحِمَهُ اللهُ to Ibn al-Qayyim رَحِمَهُ اللهُ

Shaykh al-Islam Ibn Taymiyyah رَحِمَهُ اللهُ once said to me [explaining with a metaphorical example the purpose of seeking refuge in Allah جَلَّ جَلالُهُ from Satan]: "If the shepherd's dog ever barks at you attempting to attack you, then do not engage it in a fight. Instead, turn to the shepherd and seek his help for he will leash it and save you the trouble." When a person takes refuge in Allah جَلَّ جَلالُهُ from the accursed Satan, He protects him and keeps away Satan's harm and evil from reaching him.

This shall free his heart to explore the meanings of the Quran and witness its fascinating and awe-inspiring wonders and let him collect from its treasures and gems that no eyes have ever seen, no ears have ever heard, and no mind has ever conceived. It is only his base desires and Satan that stand as a barrier between him and all these wonders because his base desires always incline towards the whispers and temptations of Satan. However, as soon as he distances himself from Satan and manages to expel him from his heart, the King takes over charge of his heart, holding it fast to the truth and reminding it of that which will assure its safety and everlasting happiness."[1]

As the slave [of Allah جَلَّ جَلالُهُ] starts to recite the Quran, he effectively begins addressing his Lord and invoking Him. Therefore, he should beware of invoking Him while his heart is busy with something else, as he will be like a man upon whom a king bestowed his favor and then granted him the permission to speak before him, but as the man

---

[1] Ibn al-Qayyim, *The Inner Dimensions of the Prayer.*

started to speak to the king he turned his back towards the king, turning his face away from him.

78

Abū Hurayrah ﷺ reported that the Messenger of Allah ﷺ said, "Charity is due for every joint of everyone, on every day the sun rises. Administering of justice between two men is charity; assisting a man to ride upon his beast or helping him load his bags upon it is charity. A good word is charity; and every step that you take towards prayer is charity, and removing harmful things from the road is charity."[1]

The Prophet's ﷺ saying "Charity is due on every joint of everyone" means that charity is due on every organ of one's body. The hadith refers to the fact that the safety and health of one's organs and body are one of the greatest favors of Allah ﷻ. Each organ needs a person to give charity for it as a way of thanking Allah ﷻ for it.

Mujāhid said, "These are the graces and favors of Allah which are very obvious so that you may thank Him." A man complained to Yūnus ibn 'Ubayd that he was very poor. Yūnus said to him, "Would you like to sell your eyesight for the amount of one hundred thousand dirhams?" The man replied, "No." Yūnus said to him, "Would you like to sell your hand for the amount of one hundred thousand dirhams?" The man replied, "No." Yūnus said to him, "Would you like to sell your legs for the amount of one hundred thousand dirhams?" The man replied, "No." Yūnus said, "I see that you have hundreds of thousands while you complain."[2]

---

[1] Recorded by al-Bukhārī and Muslim.
[2] Ibn Rajab al-Ḥanbalī, *Jāmiʿ al-ʿUlūm wa-l-Ḥikam.*

79

Bilal Assad said: "The dirtier you get the less bothered you are by dirt. The wetter you get the less bothered you are by the rain. The cleaner you are the more bothered you are by dirtiness. The drier you get the more bothered you get by the rain.

Such is the heart, the dirtier and more frequent our bad actions, the less bothered our heart's guilt is. The cleaner the actions we do, the more bothered our heart is by dirty actions. The more actions we do that connect us to materialism, the more bothered our hearts are by reminders of the Hereafter. The more actions we do that connect us to the Hereafter, the more bothered our hearts are by materialism.

People frequently complain about why they don't 'feel' their hearts connected to Allah ﷻ, and why their hearts don't 'feel' guilt by bad actions they do and know that they should be concerned. Islam is simple, it makes life simple, it makes our hearts at ease. But it's we who make it complicated on ourselves.

A simple formula we can use that the Prophet ﷺ gave to Muʿādh ؓ when he was still a young man, '... every time you commit a wrongdoing, just do a good doing after it and it will erase it ...' He asked: 'does saying 'lā ilāha illallāh' count as one those good doings?' The Prophet ﷺ replied: 'It is among the best.'[1]

The heart is the biggest trust Allah ﷻ gave us responsibility over.

Such was the dua of Prophet Ibrāhīm ﷺ:

---

[1] Sunan Aḥmad, no. 21354.

O Allah, do not make me among the losers on the day they rise, the day when wealth nor children will benefit, except the one who arrives at Allah with a heart free of defect. [The Quran, 26:88]

Yes, *īmān* rises and falls, sometimes you feel it stronger than other times. It's normal, we all go through it. But when it's consistent, we need to reflect and check ourselves."

80

You are Not Evil

You did not mean to do the wrong thing. You never thought you would end up like this. You always had your conscience, but then what happened? You experienced hurt, humiliation, degradation, violation, dismissal, disapproval, dishonesty, treachery, manipulation, control, intimidation, fear, the feeling of worthlessness and of being used. You experienced all or some or just one of those things long enough for it to make you feel like you need to break away from the prison someone kept you in. That desire to be free was justified. It was you being human, not evil.

At that moment, when you felt like you were cornered, suffocated and could not take anymore, it is at that moment that you told yourself for once, you will do what makes You happy. You will not make choices dictated by someone's influence. What took this long maybe is that you were breaking free from the one(s) who claimed to love and look out for you.

The Devil stepped in at this crucial moment. He told you it is ok to find harmless comfort in something or someone. You are not doing something *too* wrong. You are just human so it's ok. And maybe it started off as something innocent. Some kind of opportunity to breathe when the rest of life felt like you were drowning. How can you be wrong for wanting to come up for air?

But that well intentioned, only human, small step became a series of steps, even a migration, without your knowledge, away from Allah ﷻ. Your conscience, while still alive, was in coma. Your soul was there.

You were still praying. But you could not feel anything. Or even if you could feel a spiritual flicker, you could not find it in you to allow that flicker to make you change course. The Devil, and eventually you, started telling yourself you cannot help it, that you are stuck.

And so you hit rock bottom. Allah ﷻ decides to wake you up either by way of an intervention inside your heart or by a disastrous experience in your life that jolts you back. You realize you let your untamed heart choke out your soul for too long. You look back at the downward spiral and ask yourself "How was that even me?" And then you develop a kind of self-hatred. "I'm disgusting". It only increases this feeling when those who want to keep you in your downward spiral reinforce how disgusting you are the moment they notice you are about to break free.

When no one will tell you what you truly need it will be the word of Allah ﷻ, His light, that will. And you will realize that you messed up. Royally. You did evil. Terrible evil. You should be ashamed. But ashamed before Him. Resolving to change course for Him. Going through the pains of withdrawal for Him. And in that pain lies proof that you have faith, that you have good, that you are not evil, no matter what the world or your broken self tells you.

In Sūrat al-Shams [The Sun] we learn a valuable lesson:

> By the sun in its morning brightness, and by the moon as it follows it. By the day as it displays the sun's glory, and by the night as it conceals it. By the sky and how He built it, and by the earth and how He spread it, and by the soul and how He formed it and inspired it [to know] its own rebellion and piety: the one who purifies his soul succeeds and the one who corrupts it fails. [The Quran, 91:1-4]

"The conflict between day and night resembles the dark and light inside of us. The beauty of it is that even in darkness, there is a remnant of light left inside of you just like the moon in the sky during the night. You still have goodness left in you no matter what. The moon goes through phases and faith goes up and down. These struggles against our temptations and weaknesses will always be there and this is what Allah ﷻ wanted. But just as the day and night were created balanced, the soul was as well—so it doesn't tip all the way to one side. The indirect mention of balance through the sun/moon and so forth implies our ability to control ourselves is more powerful than our tendencies."[1]

[1] Bayyinah, Deeper Look.

143

81

If my Lord asks me, "Have you shyness in disobeying me? You conceal your sins from my creation—and with sins you come to me."

How will I answer? O woe to me—and who shall protect me?

I keep averting my soul with thoughts of hope—from time to time.

And I forget what is to come after death—and what is to come after I am shrouded.

As if I am guaranteed life (eternally)—and that death will not come to me.

And when the severe stupor of death overtakes me—who will protect me?

I looked at the faces; is there not from amongst them one who will ransom me?

I will be asked regarding what I have prepared in my life to save me [on the Day of Judgement].

Then how will I answer—after I have neglected my religion.

Woe to me! Did I not hear the Speech of Allah inviting me? Did I not hear what came in (the chapters of) Qāf and Yā-Sīn?

Did I not hear about the Day of Gathering, the Day of Assembling and the Day of Judgement?

Did I not hear the crier of death inviting me, calling me?

So O my Lord, a slave [turning to you] I have repented—so who then shall shelter me?

Except a Lord extensive in forgiveness—to the truth He will guide me.

I have come to you [in repentance]—so have mercy on me and make heavy my scales (with good deeds).

And lighten my account—You are the best of who will bring me to account.[1]

---

[1] Translation of a poem in Arabic that is said to have been presented to Imam Aḥmad b. Ḥanbal by a man who visited him. The poem affected the Imam greatly and made him weep.

82

"The Quran sets us up for success. It teaches us how to live accepting who we are, working through our constant mistakes, and how to healthily forgive ourselves in our coming back to Him. The Quran reminds us of the power of mindfulness. It's not necessarily a physical possession that fulfills us, but being mindful of Him as we enjoy that possession that builds fulfillment.

Imagine yourself in an ocean enjoying the calm waters. You can enjoy the swim and that was all you gained: the temporary enjoyment. But now imagine yourself immersed in an ocean He created. With every wave that hits you, you are mindful of Allah ﷻ in your life. You smile at the colors He's enabled you to see, at the moment He's allowed you to experience. Now all of a sudden, your enjoyment is permanent. It was a moment of *taqwā*, of engaging with Allah ﷻ in your mind as you enjoyed the blessing He sent you. This is a life goal: to live our lives with constant mindfulness of Him, so much so that wherever we are, we are not immersed in the blessing, but in remembering Him through that blessing."[1]

Nouman Ali Khan said, "It's to truly be in a conversation with Allah ﷻ. I will speak to Him and He will speak with me. I will speak with Him with my dua, requests, supplications, confessions, admission of where I stand, what I need, what my mistakes are, what I hope to be, how sorry I am, how I am hopeful, that He forgives me and He speaks to me: He is giving you hope, making you grateful, aware, aware of those around you, opening your eyes to reality and opening the doors of mercy on you. This conversation. This conversation will set you

---

[1] Samia Mubarak.

straight." It is being grateful to Allah ﷻ, and know Allah ﷻ, the One Who has given you each and every blessing you have or will ever have. Think of losing the ability to see. Close your eyes.

You love your child despite their mistakes. Allah ﷻ did not even scold you, or stop your heart from beating, or make you go blind after committing what is sinful, and so forth. Yet you are here still thinking that Allah ﷻ does not love you anymore? Nobody will love you like Allah ﷻ loves you. The love we already have is a gift from Allah ﷻ. The only one who thinks he is not loved is shaytan and if you do the same, whose footsteps are you following? Allah ﷻ promises to immediately respond to 'the one who calls on Me whenever they call on Me.'"[1]

A man started praying fajr in the mosque which had a ripple effect for every time he thought of doing anything unworthy or sinful, he remembered the blessing Allah ﷻ had granted him which billions of people do not possess. What we learn from this is gratitude.

Remember that He promised, "If you are thankful, I will give you more, but if you are ungrateful, My punishment is terrible indeed." [The Quran, 14:7]

"This was a manifestation of *shukr* (gratitude). That when a person does a good deed that they feel grateful for it and their gratitude manifests in them changing their lifestyle out of fear of it being squandered or disappearing. There are many of us who become spiritually stagnant because when we were blessed with favors, we did not respond with gratitude. We took them for granted. We memorized al-Baqarah, or al-Kawthar, or any chapter or verse from the book of Allah ﷻ and we did not respond with gratitude and so we didn't move

---

[1] Bayyinah, "What to Ask Allah" Khutbah.

beyond it. Allah ﷻ illuminated our hearts with the light of knowledge, but we weren't wary of sins and so that light eventually extinguished. We practiced Islam with passion and dedication and didn't realize that this was a favor that we should show gratitude for, maybe instead thinking that this was due to our own character and commitment, and so the passion calmed, and the dedication faltered. Many people see this verse and they think in terms of being thankful for physical blessings, but spiritual blessings are more worthy of being appreciated and more worthy of gratitude being shown for them."[1]

[1] Ammar Al Shukry

83

A revert to Islam asked Allah ﷻ for a sign. He thought to himself, "Allah ﷻ and I will have a conversation tonight." He wanted a sign from Allah ﷻ. He said, "I will ask for lightning." He waited. And nothing happened. He said "O Allah ﷻ I am here." As he opened the Quran where he had left off and started reading, the next ayah implied: "for those of you who ask these questions, have we not shown you enough signs?"

We say alhamdulillah, all praise and gratitude belong to Allah ﷻ. Alhamdulillah for the signs, guidance and mercy He shows us every day even when we become distant from Him, may Allah protect us from becoming distant from Him. What is alhamdulillah?

We praise Allah ﷻ. It means whenever anything good happens in this world, the only one worthy of praise is Allah ﷻ. This is the reason when the followers of Muhammad ﷺ recite this, you see the followers of Muhammad ﷺ humbled—because in every prayer they remind themselves that any good that happens is because of the goodness of Allah ﷻ, they themselves are not worthy of any praise. Any goodness that is done, it was not going to happen had it not been for the qualities of Allah's ﷻ grace, mercy, power, knowledge, and so forth.

The fact that we begin Sūrat al-Fātiḥah with this means that we are already preparing to supplicate for things, because we are in essence saying that things do not exist except for the power, might and will of Allah ﷻ, and because of that He is the only One worthy of praise. We are also saying "O Allah ﷻ we are about to ask for things on the basis that only You can give them." And Allah ﷻ decrees only good for the believer.

As Ibn Rajab al Ḥanbalī رحمه الله says: "We have to put more trust in Allah ﷻ than in what we have [of means]. This is derived from the soundness and strength of faith. Allah guaranteed the provisions of His worshippers as He says,

> There is not a creature that moves on earth whose provision is not His concern. He knows where it lives and its [final] resting place: it is all [there] in a clear record [The Quran, 11:6]"[1]

[1] Ibn Rajab al-Ḥanbalī, *Jāmi' al-'Ulūm wa-l-Ḥikam*, p. 399.

84

Never waver in your trust of Allah ﷻ who took care of you when you were only a droplet, almost non-existent.

"Why are you putting your hand on your cheek? And why are you worried?
Is your faith troubled? Why are you worried?
Why don't you leave it to Allah ﷻ? Just leave it to Allah ﷻ.
He manages and preserves our affairs while we do not know. The purpose is to save our connection with Allah ﷻ.
Do you know the little child that sleeps like a Sultan? Why? Because he has left it to his parents, he has no worries because they will take care of his needs and worries."[1]

So if you left it to Allah ﷻ, you would have the entirety of your affairs in this world and the next taken care of.

"By Allah ﷻ, there is nothing you can or should complain or worry about in this life, if you truly believe in Allah ﷻ and have certainty that we are only here to be tested for a short time, and that the purpose of our existence in life is to worship Him and to be attached to Him only. So flee and run to Allah ﷻ, and not this world; Allah ﷻ will put this world at your feet so that this world and what is in it of sustenance will run after you. Indeed, if you left the worries to our Allah ﷻ, then you will live as a king within you."[2]

[1] Jaber Al-Baghdadi.
[2] Rawan Sourchi.

85

A hundred years from today, you will be under the ground.

One hour after your funeral: the crying subsides. Your family goes home and starts to take care of your relatives' food and drink business. Meanwhile your body meets the soil.

Two hours later: there are those who call your home and make excuses for not being able to attend the funeral. Meanwhile some people at the funeral start talking about sports and politics.

After six hours: only your immediate family remains and everyone else returns home and starts planning their next day.

Twenty-four hours later: your body begins to decay; messages and calls continue from people who do not yet know you are dead.

Three days later: interviews are held for your job position to replace you.

A year later: someone says, "Wow, is that all? It's like yesterday."

It takes such short time to completely forget your existence in this world. Now reconsider the people and events that you are obsessed with today, do you think it is worth it?

"Sūrat al-Infiṭār paints this picture for us. People will finally realize. Realize what? What they put in front and what they put behind, in other words, what they made a priority and what they neglected. We constantly set priorities in life; meaning the realization of what is more important or less important—what during life mattered and affected your decision-making. Why is this question being asked? There were many times we had to pick what Allah ﷻ wanted and Him but something else became more important and took priority instead—I chose myself, my greed, someone else or their wants. No matter how much we tell ourselves that it is okay, that is us lying to ourselves. The reality of it is that when Allah ﷻ and His Messenger ﷺ tell us something, either to do something, or that something is not allowed, then they are doing it because they care for us more than we will ever care about ourselves.

> Mankind, what has lured you away [*gharra-ka*] from God? [The Quran, 82:6]

A closer look at the word *gharra* used for 'lured away' / 'deceived you' means the following: when a person puts their hopes and thoughts into something, thinking it will bring good to them. They will feel good because of it. They will be safe because of it; they will be happy because of it. All of that is wrong because it is against Allah's ﷻ commandments—in reality it is harmful. There are many things that are attractive, so we need guidance not to be drawn to everything just because it is attractive. Our heart needs guidance because it is blind without revelation. It sees something it wants and is drawn towards it. Allah ﷻ from His revelation gives vision to the heart and lets it see and think—the feeling inside of you of wanting is something Allah ﷻ put there but the way you are going about it and acting on it is wrong. The way He wants you to do it, He spelled it out for you. Shaytan comes along and says, 'Why are you so hard on yourself? Take it easy...'

Whenever we make something else a priority, Allah ﷻ gives us kindness anyway. We act as if His rules do not exist and as if they do not matter and He does not humiliate us in return. He still treats us with dignity and keeps clothes on our backs. He has always been that way. We keep overlooking Him and we do not think about it twice. On that day we do not say Allah ﷻ understands, we will then realize what deceived us. He made us perfect and shaped us and took us through phases; every event He put you through; all the people that came and left—with all those we are tested with what our priorities were. Just because Allah ﷻ is Karīm [Generous], do you think there are no consequences? Did He not tell you that the stars will fall, and the oceans will boil over?

> When the sky is torn apart, when the stars are scattered, when the seas burst forth, when graves turn inside out: each soul will know what it has done and what it has left undone. [The Quran, 82:1-5]

Did He not tell you lovingly? What did you allow to deceive you? The time to change has come, you have heard this ayah. It doesn't matter what pain you go through for the change. I would rather realize this now than on the Day of Judgement. I don't care if that makes me cry or someone else or puts me through withdrawals or someone else. I don't care how much it hurts. It doesn't matter how lazy I am, I will start praying today. People will question you when you change but you will tell them I'm setting the right priorities. The door on our deeds is not closed yet. Make a real change. You have no one to prove anything to. The only perception that matters is how you see yourself and how Allah ﷻ sees you and when that becomes clear, then you are ready for this change."[1]

---

[1] Nouman Ali Khan.

86

Every person has to experience eight things, and no one can escape from these eight:

1. Happiness and sadness

2. Meeting and separation

3. Ease and hardship

4. Good health and sickness

Sometimes you are happy and then stressed so you are surprised. Why are you surprised? This is the nature of this world [*dunyā*]. You are deluded by its pleasures, thinking it is everlasting. It never promised you that. You are to blame for thinking that. You are healthy and surprised when you are sick, why? Or when someone dies and you find out saying, "He was just twenty", "He was healthy," as if only the sick and elderly can die. Why are you surprised? Happiness and sadness, meeting and separation, difficulty and ease, and illness and wellness—this is *dunyā*.

Shaykh al-Islām Ibn Taymiyyah رَحِمَهُ اللَّه said: "A man asked one of the Salaf: 'How much Quran should we read?' He said: 'Equivalent to the amount of happiness you want'."[1] We find our refuge in Allah ﷻ, the sole refuge, and His words:

---

[1] Majmū' al-Fatāwā, 7/493.

...nor can you find any refuge except with Him. [The Quran, 18:27]

In life we experience ups and downs but through the words of Allah ﷻ, we find peace and comfort. This world was never set up for comfort, it is but a temporary stop.

Calm your mind. Give ease to your heart. Your story has been written by the One who gave you life. What is coming for you is far better than what has passed you by. Allah ﷻ is Aware of our deepest thoughts. He is All-Aware of the unspoken words in our hearts. The doubts, the fears, the worry, and the anxiety of what is to come next—put it all in His hands.

He will give to you all that your heart wants. Because Allah ﷻ sees your patience. He sees your struggle. He understands what it takes for you to hold onto the little hope you have left. He understands how you intentionally do things for His sake. Let it come how it is meant to come, by Allah's ﷻ grace. In the meantime, practice gratitude every day. The more you thank Allah ﷻ, the more He will give to you. He is with you wherever you are. And He will not leave you for a second. You are under His care, and you have been, all along.

87

How can I increase the servitude of my heart and limbs to Allah ﷻ?

"Know that the most honored part of a person is his heart. If a person has knowledge of Allah ﷻ, works for Him, strives for Him, gains nearness to Him and unveils what Allah ﷻ has, then the limbs will but follow and serve and the heart will utilize it just as kings utilize slaves."[1] We often think about why we cannot love Allah ﷻ as much as we want to, and this is because we do not appreciate Allah's ﷻ blessings upon us and take them for granted and do not realize that others have been deprived of what we have. The feeling of entitlement is contrary to thinking in a healthy way and loving Allah ﷻ.

From the story of Sulaymān ﷺ we learn that recompense is of the same nature as the righteous deed. Sulaymān ﷺ sacrificed his horses for the sake of Allah ﷻ though they were a means of transportation very dear to his heart. So Allah ﷻ rewarded him with a reward that was of the same nature as his righteous deed; a far superior means of transportation, the wind. By the same token, one who lowers his gaze and sacrifices the pleasure of looking at the impermissible, Allah ﷻ would reward them with a reward of the same nature, which might be a wife or children that will be the coolness of his eyes. Another example could be a person who guards his tongue and refuses to let himself speak of matters of no concern to him. Allah ﷻ would reward them with making his heart able to speak wisdom in situations when trials strike.

[1] Aḥmad ibn Qudāmah al-Maqdisī, *Discipline: The Path to Spiritual Growth.*

88

Allah ﷻ often chooses us to be the light in the darkness. We are placed in environments where we are the lamp that lights up the darkness around us. There is peace in knowing that Allah ﷻ has chosen you in the midst of such environments to be the lighthouse to guide others. All of us go through these situations.

Allah ﷻ could have sent Ibrāhīm ﷺ to any environment but he was sent to the hub, the capital, of *shirk* [idolatry, the association of partners with Allah ﷻ]. He had to see the falsehood and question things to see the light. He was alone in speaking the truth and was not afraid of those who might come after him. Ibrāhīm ﷺ looked at everything and saw a contradiction between what he saw, which was the Oneness of Allah ﷻ in everything, and what his nation was doing. There are important lessons to learn from our father, Ibrāhīm ﷺ:

- Ibrāhīm ﷺ knew that the King of Kings is Allah ﷻ and that nothing happens without His command. Everything is governed by Allah ﷻ. When we internalize this, then we become of those who can say "I don't have to succumb to the authority of anyone if everything is controlled by Allah ﷻ—I have to surrender to Allah ﷻ, no one else." We are not swayed by societal forces around us. Your environment becomes irrelevant when you have a firm conviction in Allah ﷻ. He left a legacy behind for us not to be followers of society. It is to commit to the truth regardless of everything else.

- When you know clearly that this is what Allah ﷻ wants, nothing will get in the way. Two emotions to get away from are fear [of enemies, the future, or loss and sadness [being afraid of sadness for oneself or others]. Ibrāhīm ﷺ gave up the safety of his family. Is it easy to be kicked out and not know where you will eat next, leaving the only home and relatives you have known? To have conviction no matter what my feelings tell me because I know Allah ﷻ will take care of me, that is the way of Ibrāhīm ﷺ. The Quran describes them as great emotions. Ibrāhīm ﷺ crushed the idea that it might hurt someone's feelings. If Allah ﷻ wants this, then it must be better and Allah ﷻ can never mean harm.

- No matter how impossible it seems Allah ﷻ will provide and take care of me. Shaytan promises bankruptcy. We must not stay silent when something wrong is said. We should speak lovingly like Ibrāhīm ﷺ. Your parents, children, spouse, relatives, if these are dearer to you than Allah ﷻ and his Messenger ﷺ, then punishment awaits.

- Allah ﷻ is the protective friend and always accompanies those who believe. We demonstrate to Allah ﷻ what we are willing to do for Him, and He is there always protecting us.

- Our faith in Allah ﷻ allows us to internally have peace in any situation. The world outside has an effect on us but what is happening inside of us also has an impact on the outside, faith maximizes the impact of the inside and minimizes how the outside affects us.

- Faith is three things:
  - Absolute hope in Allah ﷻ, you are never alone— Ibrāhīm ﷺ is the most lonely person, abandoned by everyone in his community but he is not alone. He has Allah ﷻ. We know with conviction that Allah ﷻ will compensate us for our efforts, our losses and our sacrifices.

o Dependence on Allah 𝕏, being vulnerable with Him. Allah 𝕏 will still care and will not care less no matter what. He knows us from the depths of our souls, and yet still guides, cares for us and provides for us.

o Surrender to Allah 𝕏—as humans we want to be in control of our lives. Surrendering to Allah 𝕏 means He will take care of the rest. He controls the means and the ends. Allah 𝕏 will sort it out. You surrender your strategy, course of action, and everything else to Allah 𝕏 and thereafter you do not worry about consequences because they are in Allah's 𝕏 hands.

- The dimension at the center of Ibrāhīm's discourse 𝕏 is the love and care of Allah 𝕏. I am abandoning all of you and I will get away from whatever you are calling on and I am just going to call my Master, and my hope is that I never become miserable and hopeless when calling on my Master. No matter how bad the situation gets, my hope in Allah 𝕏 should never change. Allah 𝕏 has rewarded him far into the future and long after he is gone, for there are millions loyal to him. He was willing to leave everything and everyone he loved because he left them for the sake of Allah 𝕏.

- He knows Allah will feed him and will help him through anything. Everything we have, have ever had, is from Allah. Allah has given us all we have. Even our house. On the outside yes, our parents gave us our house but in reality it is Allah. Being able to benefit from the food, the food being able to go down your throat, it is Allah. He continues to heal me. Ibrahim had this level of trust in Allah at the worst time of his life.

There is a calmness that comes from letting go. From letting Allah take over.[12]

[1] Bayyinah, Deeper Look, Āl ʿImrān.
[2] Ibid, Our Father Ibrahim Series.

89

Allah ﷻ is the easiest One to please and the people are the hardest to please, yet we chase the acceptance of people our whole lives. Allah ﷻ gives us more freedom than any human can give us. Whatever you do for Allah ﷻ, you will be compensated for, but the same does not necessarily apply to humans. The ultimate goal should be Allah ﷻ being content with you because things come and go. Allah ﷻ is the ultimate goal. Allah ﷻ created you and everything you chase too. It is not yours to begin with. Everything belongs to Allah ﷻ. Allah ﷻ purifies us of our environments, so that we can truly find the company of Allah ﷻ.

We debase ourselves into the lowest of low by engaging in our desires and attempting to please other than Allah ﷻ. The Devil wants us to seek our validation with other than Allah ﷻ, when Allah ﷻ is the only One that should be sought, for how could you give yourself up to your sworn enemy so casually?

Divorce this worldly life as ʿAlī ibn Abī Ṭālib ؓ said: "I divorce you O worldly life (*dunyā*) three times irrevocably."

"O you who severed the connection to his Lord, return. O you who vowed to reject his Lord, repent. You were honored when Iblīs [Satan] was ordered to prostrate to you, whereas Iblīs was cast out when he refused to do so. Yet I truly wonder at you! How could you, despite that, make reconciliation with the Devil and spurn your Lord? How ruined you are, for your status in the Eyes of your Lord is greater than the status of the Night of Power (i.e., *Laylat al-Qadr*)."[1]

---

[1] Ibn al-Jawzī, *Seeds of Admonishment and Reform*, p. 108.

Fearing Allah ﷻ, the Most High, is the key to pleasing Allah ﷻ. Ibn al-Jawzī رَحِمَهُ ٱللَّٰه remarks, "If he [the devotee] feels he is veiled [from his Lord], he weeps for being distanced from his Lord, and if the gate of acceptance is opened for him, he fears being expelled."[1]

---

[1] Ibid., p. 71.

90

The Permanent Departure[1]

Insofar as your stay in this world is temporary, you must always be ready for a permanent departure. This form of readiness comes as a mindset; it becomes manifest only when denouncement defines you in relation to life. To believe that it is not possessing wealth that makes you wealthy but rather denouncing wealth; that it is not claiming power that makes you powerful, but rather denouncing power. With such a mindset you are the wealthiest man without possessing any wealth other than the wisdom of denouncing it; you are the most powerful man without exerting power over any man other than yourself—to have the power to own your perception on life. Hence, to the extent that you are willing to stay the course of life, it is you who does the world a favor and not otherwise. Acquire the wisdom to be at peace with the fact of departing from this life [by being absolutely indifferent]; then you will be in peace with the totality of the facts that constitute this life, and nothing could possibly disturb this peace.

To be ready for such departure, we must ready ourselves and the state of our heart. Remembrance [*dhikr*] Purifies and Polishes the Heart.

Our Prophet ﷺ said: "For everything there is a polish, and the polish of the heart is the remembrance of Allah [ﷻ]."[2]

Ibn al-Qayyim رحمه الله explains that the heart rusts like copper and silver. And as it can rust, it can also be polished. Through *dhikr*, the

[1] Dr Mohammed Ali.
[2] Al-Bayhaqī.

heart can shine like a crystal mirror. Thus, when one neglects *dhikr*, the heart rusts, and when one remembers Allah ﷻ, it shines. There are two things which cause a heart to rust: heedlessness (*ghaflah*) and sin. Conversely, the heart can be polished by two things: remembrance (*dhikr*) and seeking forgiveness.

Doing *dhikr* purifies us from our sins and protects us from the Devil. Both sins and the Devil are the root causes of our worldly anxieties, unhappiness, and stress. Thus, the more we remember Allah ﷻ, the happier and the more content we will be. The more grateful we are, and the more we find things to be grateful for, the happier and more at peace we can be.

91

A glimpse of the dua of the different Prophets of Allah ﷻ teaches us valuable and timeless lessons. The dua is the believer's most powerful tool.[1]

The dua of Mūsā ﷺ: "My Lord! I am truly in desperate need of whatever good You may have in store for me." [The Quran, 88:24]

We have to have pure intentions and expect nothing in return for what we do from people except from Allah ﷻ. We should do it for Allah ﷻ. Though he was a fugitive, had no food, shelter, etc., he still thanked Allah ﷻ for what he had already sent him and said I desperately need it. Essentially, what Allah ﷻ has given you is what you need the most and the best for you. *Faqīr* [used in this verse] is the worst possible situation, but the *miskīn* [used elsewhere in the Quran] might at least own something, as evident in Sūrat al-Kahf—owning a ship.

So Mūsā ﷺ is saying, I have got nothing. 'Ya Allah ﷻ, I acknowledge that I have absolutely nothing. And I don't even have a means to earn anything. You are the only one who sent this down my way; I am not going to complain.' A *faqīr* is also someone whose backbone is broken. You can't lift anything; things have to be given to you because you can't even get them. 'Ya Allah ﷻ whatever you sent towards me is because I'm *faqīr*, I can't go and get it. You are bringing it to me.' Mūsā ﷺ was given a job, shelter, and the daughter's hand in marriage just because he appreciated Allah's ﷻ blessings when he had nothing.

[1] Bayyinah, Ramadan Gems.

Mūsā's second dua ﷺ: Mūsā said, 'Lord, lift up my heart and ease my task for me.' [The Quran, 20:25-26]

It means you're not nervous, anxious, angry, bothered, but rather calm. Another meaning: keep me brave because in life, massive tasks intimidate us, which leads to the tightness of our chests. Before anything you do, the state of your heart matters. When we ask Allah ﷻ to expand our heart, we are asking for Allah ﷻ for more Quran to be in our hearts because that is how Allah ﷻ expanded the breast of our Messenger ﷺ. The purpose of revelation is to lighten your burden. And after that he asks: make my task easy. He knows no task is easy unless Allah ﷻ makes it easy. Allah ﷻ tells us if your chest is full of light and in the right place, everything else becomes easy.

92

The Dua of Yūsuf 🕊: 'I seek refuge with Allah! My master has been good to me; wrongdoers never prosper.' She made for him, and he would have succumbed to her if he had not seen evidence of his Lord—We did this in order to keep evil and indecency away from him, for he was truly one of Our chosen servants. [The Quran, 12:23-24]

Something stopped him. He saw the glaring evidence from his Master. It was the knowledge he had in his heart. When you think of something, it is in your brain, but when you see something, it is in front of you. Sometimes you know right or wrong but because it is not in front of you, you do not see it that moment. The remembrance should be so strong it should be like a curtain coming between us and what is sinful. Believers see what others cannot see ('It's good, go for it, it's nice, just have some fun') and we do not fall into these traps because we have evidence from our master even though our biological makeup and feelings will want to see things a certain way, we have to go against it. You see evidence from your master that stops you from eating in Ramadan food that otherwise would be halal for you. You have a label due to evidence from your master how to see things. No one is immune. The formula of divine intervention: when someone can see the evidence of their Master and they are able to stop themselves at that moment when it is tempting; if you can do that Allah 🕊 will steer away evil and shamelessness away from you [in the heart]. 'This is how we pushed him away from evil.' Allah 🕊 will put force fields in your heart and take you away from evil thoughts.

He says ma'ādhallāh—I seek refuge with Allah 🕊 [cling on to Allah 🕊]. This is more emphatic, and there is no other [form] of seeking Allah's 🕊 seeking protection more powerful than this in an emergency. He is screaming to Allah ﷻ: take me somewhere I can hold on to you [take refuge in you]. I am not asking only for protection but asking for escape. Then he says Allah ﷻ has provided for me all along: if I commit this crime is like I'm letting go of Allah ﷻ. He has done too much good for me. He recognizes this crime will hurt his faith and will take him away from Allah's ﷻ protection. The Devil is pulling you and you hold on to Allah ﷻ. You undo it. They realize they cannot do it without Allah ﷻ. Servitude is realizing our powerlessness. How can he fight such temptation? When people do their very best, they are given strength and willpower to do the right thing. I always trusted Allah ﷻ in doing the best for me no matter what, so I know Allah ﷻ will help me and be there for me in the best way possible. I don't let my outside conditions (health, physical condition, or economic condition) define that Allah ﷻ is doing this to me or that Allah ﷻ is good/bad to me—Allah ﷻ is always the best to me. I don't look at these shallow metrics to see how Allah ﷻ has been to me. How do I know Allah ﷻ is good to me? Because I do my very best and Allah ﷻ gives me sense to do the right thing and won't let me forget Him.

Yūsuf's ﷺ second dua: "My master is dearer to me from what these women are calling me to do." [The Quran, 12:33]

He is not asking for jail. He has two options. Jail or sin. He has to pick. He is not asking Allah ﷻ about the limited options he has and takes one not to disobey Allah ﷻ. Allah ﷻ gives to whomever He wills and whoever relies upon Him. Ya Allah ﷻ if you don't get me away from their scheming, I might become victim to it. If you find yourself in an environment, you will soon find many things becoming normal to you and take shape in you; more stuff becomes normal and obedience to Allah ﷻ becomes harder. Naturally our heart wants to obey Allah ﷻ but when we put ourselves in sinful environments our nature changes. Allah ﷻ answered his prayer, got him away from their scheming. He is the One who hears and knows. When you find yourself like this, then Allah 🙵 hears you. So we have to be brave enough to ask Allah 🙵 from the heart that we prefer pain to sinning and then Allah 🙵 will save us. When you show Allah 🙵, He will rescue you.

Dua of Ayyūb 🙵: 'Indeed, distress has befallen me, and You are the Most Merciful of the merciful.' [The Quran, 21:83†]

What little we do know about him is that he became extremely sick. The first thing to note is that people cannot function and have normal lives (drive, study, go out) when they become sick, and as a result people feel useless—turns people into pessimists (they feel Allah 🙵 does not care for them because they think I can't be productive and if Allah 🙵 loved me I would be productive). In that state he calls on Allah 🙵. He is saying I have been barely touched by harm. As hard my life can be there is much greater harm that Allah 🙵 prevents from me. Compared to the harm Allah 🙵 protects me from, this is just a touch. If I got cut off from Allah 🙵, that is the ultimate harm. Compared to that, this is nothing. He is also saying my inability is starting to affect me. He is saying it has started to affect my heart. Before it gets worse, he says You are the one who cares and loves more than anyone. The child doesn't even need to say they need food because the one that loves the child (the mother) will do what needs to be done out of love anyway. You don't have to make a request. As a result of this statement, which was not even a request, Allah 🙵 alleviated every harm from him, not just his sickness.

93

Dua of Sulaymān ﷺ: 'My master empower me [*awzi'-nī*] to be grateful for your favor that you have done to me and empower me to grateful for the favor You have done to both my parents.' [The Quran, 27:19]

Being overjoyed over any success is okay, but it is actually what's going on in the heart that Allah ﷻ checks. Sulaymān ﷺ is happy. There is a kind of happiness that is okay and a kind that isn't. This is balanced in Sulaymān's ﷺ dua.

Awzi'-nī is from *waz'*: soldiers organized perfectly, mustered and gathered; to push someone forward (this goes back to discipline); finally, to make someone passionate/obsessed with something. We translated it as "empower" but it actually means gather every ounce of strength, talent, and focus I have ya rabb and turn them into being grateful to you. When there is a lot on your mind, you can forget sometimes. So, he asks Allah ﷻ, to gather his focus to be grateful. Successful people forget who brings about these successes.

He adds *wālidayya* ["my parents"]: be grateful to both your parents [Allah ﷻ says]. One test to see how grateful you are to Allah ﷻ, is to ask yourself any good that your parents have done that you are grateful for. This is a core part of being grateful to Allah ﷻ. Our parents raised us when we were nothing. If Allah ﷻ had not guided our parents we would not have been raised Muslims. Even if they did one thing good, to acknowledge it is incumbent upon you. When you become successful it is easy to be bad because no one can question you. The dua asks for all his power and influence to be used for the sake of Allah ﷻ, for good. Give me ability to do good that you are happy with.' Good deeds are already what Allah ﷻ is happy with, so why add that

You are happy with? Sometimes we do good things people acknowledge but even if everyone is acknowledging it, in my heart I am not attributing those opportunities to Allah ﷻ—thinking I have done these good deeds, etc. Those good deeds mean nothing if they don't make Allah ﷻ happy.

Two things happen when we do good deeds: either people appreciate you or no one appreciates you. In both cases you are looking for acknowledgment somewhere else. Appreciation from people should not encourage us and lack of appreciation should not discourage us. We do this for Allah ﷻ. He says ya Allah ﷻ join me with your righteous slaves. Give me special mercy of yours and allow me the privilege to be around those—he understands those are the real VIPs. The more you are with these good people, the more you appreciate more things and become more grateful.

94

The dua of our Prophet ﷺ that Allah ﷻ instructed him to make: 'Say, 'My Lord, make me go in truthfully, and come out truthfully, and grant me a supporting authority from You." [The Quran, 17:80]

Allow me to enter an entrance of truth and allow me to exit with an exit of truth. Every time something bad happens, think of the entrance into a blessing. If you will ever put me in any situation, I want to make sure I go into that situation with truth (because I was truthful, I enter this situation); give me an environment which allows me to remain committed to the truth. Whether I leave or exit, allow me to hold on to the truth. We fall into and out of situations and in any of them we are begging Allah ﷻ no matter what any of that happens, 'Ya Allah ﷻ don't let my commitment to the truth waver. As long my commitment to the truth is there, I don't mind.' The dua says 'O Allah (ﷻ) give me power and strength so that I can remain committed to the truth,' because it is very hard. Allah ﷻ has to help. This is captured in *ladun-ka sulṭānan naṣīrā* ["a supporting authority from You"]—something that only comes from you O Allah [ﷻ].

The second dua of our Prophet ﷺ: 'Al-'Abbās ؓ, the uncle of the Prophet ﷺ, came to the Prophet [ﷺ] and said 'Ya Rasulullah, teach me a dua.' The Prophet ﷺ said: "O my uncle, say: O Allah, I ask you for *'āfiyah*"[1]. Now what is *'āfiyah*?

To save me from any afflictions.

To be healthy, you are in *'āfiyah*.

---

[1] *Riyāḍ al-Ṣāliḥīn; Sunan al-Tirmidhī.*

173

To have enough money, you are in *'āfiyah.*

To live, you are in *'āfiyah.*

To have your children protected, you are in *'āfiyah.*

And if you are forgiven and not punished, you are in *'āfiyah.*

So basically *'āfiyah* means: 'O Allah, protect me from any pain and suffering.' This includes both worlds. 'Al-'Abbās ﷺ thought about this and came back after a few days and said (paraphrased): 'Ya Rasulullah, this dua seems a little short. I want something great.' The Prophet ﷺ said: 'My dear uncle, ask Allah for *'āfiyah* for *wallahi*, you cannot be given anything better than *'āfiyah.*' It is a simple dua. Sincerely mean what you say while praying. 'O Allah, I ask You to be saved from any distress, grief, hardship, harm, don't test me, etc.'¹

¹ "The shortest most powerful prayer", *The Ideal Student.*

95

... and provides for them from sources they could never imagine. And whoever puts their trust in Allah, then He alone is sufficient for them. Certainly Allah achieves His Will. Allah has already set a destiny for everything. [The Quran, 65:3]

Yasir Qadhi said: "Sometimes, when you were least expecting it, a turn unexpectedly appears on your roadmap, confusing you. Those of faint heart assume they are lost or must go back to the beginning. Skeptics stop proceeding, wondering where this path came from and what went wrong. Those who put their trust in Allah ﷻ go forth, understanding that Allah ﷻ is guiding them to a better path and a higher goal.

There are times that we are so blind to the path we are on that we don't really stop to think about where it is leading us. So, Allah ﷻ blesses us by placing an obstacle in our path, thereby guiding us to another path. Hasn't the past already taught us that each and every obstacle in our lives eventually turned out for the best? Then why is it that every time another obstacle comes, we doubt and lose faith? Truly, it is possible that you do not like something, yet Allah ﷻ will place much good in it. Alhamdulillah for Islam."

> Fighting has been made obligatory upon you believers, though you dislike it. Perhaps you dislike something which is good for you, and like something which is bad for you. Allah knows and you do not know." [The Quran, 2:216]

"The problems we face in life are not stop signs. They're the Almighty's way of making us learn. So use them as guidelines to move forward. The Almighty may test you to see if you're really true to your word or do you just pay lip service. Do your actions speak as loud as your words?

Practice what you preach, and He will raise you in status. Don't rely on others to make you happy. Be positive. The Almighty is by your side. Take care of your mindset. He will make you confident. There's beauty in pain. We connect better with the Almighty when we're in pain than when we're content. That's how He draws us closer. Never tire of telling the Almighty your problems. He cares, He listens, He understands, and He doesn't give up on you; unlike some people. To fail doesn't make you a failure. It teaches and reminds you that the Almighty's Plan always prevails. He'll send you signs and redirect you!"[1]

[1] Mufti Menk, Motivational Moments II compilation.

96

Allah ﷻ speaks before we make dua, He wants us to know something. Allah ﷻ does not put a burden on anyone beyond their capacity:

1. Everyone has different capacities and responsibilities. Allah ﷻ does not ask us beyond our capability. He knows our capacities and capabilities.

2. If Allah ﷻ gave you any responsibility, then you are capable of it.

3. Allah ﷻ does not hold you responsible except to your potential. Allah ﷻ gave us extensive potential. Allah ﷻ will ask you, "I gave you this much potential, did you exhaust it?" Work in the way Allah ﷻ shaped you and formed you. Everything you do in life, do the very best in and not just to get by. This is Allah's ﷻ expectation of the believers.

Every individual will benefit from what they earn and be harmed by what they have earned. Different people make different excuses (i.e., "You pray five times a day? I could never do that!"). They are not realizing that Allah ﷻ has said the exact opposite. He would not give these obligations if in His wisdom He knew we were unable to perform them. Sometimes people are pressured and made to feel bad about making the right choices; leading often to the disobedience of Allah ﷻ to please people or avoid displeasing them. Allah ﷻ says no one takes the burden of others. Your burden is yours. Their burden is theirs. All you can do is what Allah ﷻ has told you. People will make you think that you are causing them pain, etc., but it is themselves who are responsible.

We remind ourselves that an easy attack of shaytan is forgetfulness [such as by making us miss prayers]. But more than that is when he makes you forget your purpose. You are made for a higher purpose; He has His reasons when He placed you in this family, gave you wealth or not, made your homeland this particular country, gave you knowledge.

> God does not burden any soul with more than it can bear: each gains whatever good it has done, and suffers its bad. "Lord, do not take us to task if we forget or make mistakes. Lord, do not burden us as You burdened those before us. Lord, do not burden us with more than we have strength to bear. Pardon us, forgive us, and have mercy on us. You are our Protector, so help us against the disbelievers." [The Quran, 2:286]

Beg Allah ﷻ not to let us fail like the people of the past. I am not confident. I do not want to be tested. I may fail. We should worry and contemplate so that Allah ﷻ does not do that to us by allowing us to be put in unbearable situations.

97

When you go through personal trials, loss of wealth, poverty, and depression, sit alone and diagnose the problem. Why, what did I do? When the ummah is massacred and at the same time Allah ﷻ promised us victory, we have to ask why. Why did this happen to us?

When a business makes losses, board members gather together and try to determine what went wrong and how to prevent it from happening again. In the same way, we have to hold our lives accountable so we can diagnose the sin that caused our difficulties and ask for forgiveness. Many verses tell us that whatever befalls us is due to our own sins. We only get defeated from our own faults. When we leave guidance and go on our own, we become the lowest of the low and get humiliated. When the law of Allah ﷻ is implemented on earth then victory comes from Allah ﷻ. Victory is always achieved through Allah ﷻ.

We must run back to Allah ﷻ, and seek our refuge with Allah ﷻ, the sole refuge. To take refuge we must cling onto Allah ﷻ firmly just as algae clings onto rocks refusing to let go, or like meat to bone.

The meaning of *a'ūdhu* [in *a'ūdhu bi-llāh*, "I seek refuge in Allah"] is I seek refuge, guard myself and take precaution. There are two opinions concerning the basis of this verb. The first is that it is derived from the meaning of *al-satar*, covering or protection, and the second is that it is derived from the meaning of *lugum al-mujawara*, firmly adhering to that which adjoins it[1]. As for the first opinion then the Arabs used to say with regards to a house that is in the shade of a tree *'uwwadh.*

[1] Al-Rāzī, vol. 1, p. 70; in 'Ādil, vol. 1, p. 94.

The same applies to the one who takes refuge, for he seeks protection and cover from his enemy with the one he seeks refuge with. As for the second opinion, then the Arabs used to say regarding flesh that was stuck to a bone and could not be removed, *'uwwadha*, because of its refusal to be dislodged from it. The same applies to the one taking refuge for he sticks firmly to the one he is seeking refuge with and refuses to be distanced. Both opinions are correct, for both include seeking refuge. The one taking refuge seeks protection with the one he is seeking refuge with and sticks firmly to him. His heart attaches itself to him and holds firm just as the child sticks close to its father when threatened by an enemy.

98

Ibn Qudāmah mentioned in his book *Al-Tawwābīn*, on the authority of 'Abd al-Wāḥid b. Zayd, that he said: "We were on a ship and the wind dragged us to an island, so we went out and found in it a man worshipping an idol. We approached him and said, 'O man, whom do you worship?' He pointed out to an idol. We said, 'We have on the ship someone who can make something like that [an idol], so this is not a Lord to worship.' He said, 'Whom do you worship?' We replied, 'We worship Allah ﷻ.' He asked, 'What is Allah [ﷻ]?' We answered, 'The One Whose Throne is above the heavens, His authority on earth, and in the dead and the living His decree.'

He asked, 'And how did you come to know about him?' We said, 'This Great King, this praiseworthy Creator, sent to us a noble messenger who informed us of this.' He said, 'What did the messenger do?' We said, 'He conveyed the message then Allah ﷻ caused him to die.' He said: 'Did he not leave a sign amongst you?' We replied, 'Yes.' He said, 'What did he leave?' We said, 'He left a Book from The King [Allah ﷻ]. He said: "Show me the book of The King, for the books of kings are supposed to be good.' We brought the Quran to him, and he said, 'I do not know it.'

We recited upon him a surah from the Quran, and as we were reciting, he was crying, he kept crying until we finished the surah. Then he said: 'The One whom these words belong to is not supposed to be disobeyed.' Then he became Muslim, so we taught him the legislation of Islam, some surahs and we took him with us to the ship. When we left, it became dark so each of us headed towards his bed, The man said, 'O people, this God whom you guided me to, when it becomes dark does he sleep?' We said, 'No, slave of Allah ﷻ, He is The Great ever living, He does not sleep.' Upon hearing that he said: 'Woe to you, what kind of slaves are you? You sleep while your Lord does not?' And he left us and stayed up worshipping Allah 🕮. When we reached our land, I said to my companions: This man is new to Islam and a stranger in this land, so we gathered for him some money and gave it to him. He said, 'What is this?' We replied, 'To use it to get your necessities.' He said, '*Lā ilāha illa 'llāh*! I was on an island in the middle of the sea worshipping an idol apart from Him [Allah 🕮] and He did not leave me or abandon me, so is He going to abandon me now after I have come to know Him?' Then he left seeking provisions on his own, and was from the great righteous people until he died ..."[1]

---

[1] Ibn Qudāmah, *Al-Tawwābīn*.

99

Ibn al-Jawzī رَحِمَهُ اللهُ said: "By Allah ﷻ, if you do not endure the bitterness of medicine in your throat you shall never be assured of even a tiny bit of good health in your body. The troops of your desires have housed themselves inside yourself, fortifying the fortress of lassitude and negligence. So charge with the soldiers of piety with the swords of strong will-power drawn out and storm their gates! ... Though you rush to join the fight, but you are not actually taking a side in the battle. You would like to reach the loftiest ranks, though you have not yet taken one step upon the staircase of struggling and striving! How is that you wait for the harvest when you have not even planted any seeds?"[1]

"How many of us voluntarily inflict ourselves with pain we can see the benefit of? We lift weights, climb mountains, push ourselves into physically and mentally exhausting careers, and so much more. We willingly take ourselves to these places of pain and hardship, but we endure the repercussions because we can see the end result. We'll be more fit, stronger, richer, or protected. Yet for some reason, when the hardship arrives at our door without personal choice, we are suddenly at dismay and thrown into panic.

It's as if we can comfortably rely on our own very limited choices yet question what has arrived from the Divine planner. Can an obstacle thrown at your door not be a means of gaining strength and protection? Without a doubt. We become so consumed by the hardship we didn't plan for that we can no longer see the possibly very fruitful end results. If only we can trust the One who puts us in

---

[1] Ibn al-Jawzī, *Seeds of Admonishment and Reform*, pp. 56-57.

situations to strengthen us as much as we trust ourselves that a grueling bike ride will give us the outcome we're looking for."[1]

Mufti Menk similarly said, "When you submit fully to the Almighty, don't be surprised if He tests you with tough times and challenges. These are the things that bring you closer to Him. Show Him sincerely that you're worthy of His Paradise! The Almighty does not consider you superior because of your rank or riches. He looks at your heart, level of piety and your closeness to Him; and don't forget whatever position you have in life, be humble. Don't compare yourself to others. It's the Almighty who raises you, not people around you!"[2]

[1] Samia Mubarak.
[2] Mufti Menk, Motivational Moments II.

100

The only two relationships that will last with you forever and ever are: your relationship with Allah ﷻ and your relationship with yourself. Make sure to foster and strengthen these relationships to the best of your ability; maybe even at the cost of giving up on some others sometimes. These are the truest ones you are going to have in your lifetime. Do not look elsewhere when you have these. Anything beyond will simply be an add-on and blessing from Allah ﷻ and you can ask Him for it. You can have them, always and anytime, as long as you put in effort to nourish and develop them strong and stronger with each passing day.

'Abd al-Raḥmān al-Sa'dī رحمه الله said: "And beware of feeling regret over past affairs which were not decreed for you, or loss of health, wealth, a job and the likes. Let your focus and concern be rectifying the actions of the day you are in; for indeed a person is the offspring of their day—they do not grieve over the past, nor do they look distantly into the future where it is of no benefit to them.

And be truthful, fulfill your oaths and promises and be just in all of your dealings. Give people their rights in full and in abundance. Do so, with a soul at peace and an *īmān* that is truthful and sincere. And busy yourself with your own shortcomings and your own affairs above the shortcomings and affairs of others.

And deal with every individual person according to what is appropriate for their mental state; whether young or old, male, or female, the ruling class or the ruled. Be gentle and merciful with every individual—even the wild or domesticated animals. Verily Allah ﷻ is Merciful only to His Slaves who show mercy. Strive constantly in all your endeavors and affairs. Keep your mind open to any and every benefit—whether religious or worldly."[1]

[1] *Majmū' Mu'allafātihi,* 21/258.

IOI

"When your child lashes out at you, when you raise your voice to distract yourself from the real pain overwhelming your heart, consider how Adam ﷺ and Eve could have possibly felt emotionally when they realized one of their sons had killed their other. Or how Ya'qūb ﷺ reacted when his other children had dropped his blessed son, their brother Joseph ﷺ, down a well. Or the tears in Nūḥ's ﷺ heart as his son was overcome by waves as he watched, helpless, unable to save him because of his own child's refusal. When you're struggling in your relationship with your parents, think of Abraham ﷺ and his father. When you long for and miss your late parents, think about Muhammad ﷺ crying at the grave of his mother.

When you're worried about what others may say about you or someone you love, consider Maryam, peace be upon her, approaching her shocked people with a baby; trusting that God would be her supporter. When you struggle with being a single mom or a single dad, think about the mother of Jesus ﷺ. When you weep over the one person who you thought would be your supporter, consider the pain Lūṭ ﷺ must have felt because of the actions of his wife.

When the one person whom you wanted to love you, to be in love with you, to build their life with you, can never be who you thought they could be and instead harm and oppress you, remember Āsiya, wife of the tyrannical Pharaoh, who called out, 'My Lord, build for me near You a house in Paradise!' Each one of our heroes (may Allah's ﷺ peace be upon them all) had to trust that Allah ﷺ would be with them in the struggles of this life with their loved ones, and in the next. As Mūsā ﷺ said when his people spoke of abandonment:

'Indeed, my Lord is with me, and He will guide me.' [The Quran, 26:62]

And Allah ﷻ did guide him. Just as he had promised him and his brother. And He will be with us. Beyond relationships, struggles, pain, concern, longing, and heartbreak, whatever we have, will end but Allah ﷻ remains. He hasn't gone anywhere. If you want Him back in your life, to help you deal and heal, know that He is ready for you, as He was there for them, even when those who should have been there weren't. Find your peace in The Peace. Turn to Him."[1]

---

[1] Ustadha Maryam Amir.

102

The mercy of Allah ﷻ in not letting us know the future

"How many of us would shy away from our dreams knowing that we would inevitably fail? How many of us would escape the idea of love knowing that we would inevitably lose it? How many of us would not study, or have children, or embark on a journey, knowing that these things would bring us much pain? We would live small, simple lives. We would never try, never climb, never soar.

I've heard many people lamenting over their situations saying, "If only I had known"—but if you had "known" what hardships would come, you wouldn't have ever striven to do something and be someone better. You wouldn't have done anything. You would have sat at home, feeble and crippled by fear. The pain hurts, yes. The failure stings, yes. The bottom where you've fallen has scraped you deeply, yes. You may look into the mirror and no longer recognize yourself from the wounds that now line your heart. But healing is beautiful, and success comes after failure. And when you are at the bottom, you learn how to build up better than before. You may not know it now, but the awkward and imperfect scabs and scars on your heart make it beautiful. How Merciful a Lord to not let us know our futures. He is Merciful to let us fail, and Merciful to let us lose, and Merciful to let us feel pain. It is only because of this Mercy that we are able to try and strive and attempt love and happiness. Alhamdulillah."[1]

You are tested, not by what you can do with ease or in times of ease, but what you do with difficulty. Your kindness towards the one who

---

[1] From "A Temporary Gift: Reflections on Love, Loss, and Healing."

hurts you; your generosity when giving more than you have; your patience in all hardships; your acceptance of people no matter their judgments; your calm when provoked; your hand to the one who bites back; your strength to get back up when you are knocked down, to the simplest smile on the most difficult of days. Such attributes can only be genuine when reciprocity [or lack thereof] does not influence them. No gains, just a pure heart.

You need trials to wake up sometimes and to bring your heart to where it should be in terms of your relationship with Allah ﷻ. Allah ﷻ is stitching all these events together and I do not know how they fit into the larger plan, but He knows better. He wants to test if you will really hold on to Him despite the hardship and pain.

103

And Muhammad ﷺ was like the dawn to the worlds sent by Allah ﷻ as a mercy for this world and the next. Wonder at this narration of the intercession of our beloved Prophet ﷺ:

"Then I will ask for my Lord's permission, and it will be given, and then He will inspire me to praise Him with such praises as I do not know now. So I will praise Him with those praises and will fall down, prostrate before Him. Then it will be said, 'O Muhammad, raise your head and speak, for you will be listened to; and ask, for your will be granted [your request]; and intercede, for your intercession will be accepted.' I will say, 'O Lord, my followers! My followers!' And then it will be said, 'Go and take out of the Hellfire all those who have faith in their hearts, equal to the weight of a barley grain.' I will go and do so and return to praise Him with the same praises and fall down [prostrate] before Him.

Then it will be said, 'O Muhammad, raise your head and speak, for you will be listened to, and ask, for you will be granted [your request]; and intercede, for your intercession will be accepted.' I will say, 'O Lord, my followers! My followers!' It will be said, 'Go and take out of it all those who have faith in their hearts equal to the weight of a small ant or a mustard seed.' I will go and do so and return to praise Him with the same praises and fall down in prostration before Him. It will be said, 'O, Muhammad, raise your head and speak, for you will be listened to, and ask, for you will be granted [your request]; and intercede, for your intercession will be accepted.' I will say, 'O Lord, my followers!' Then He will say, 'Go and take out [all those] in whose hearts there is faith even to the lightest, lightest mustard seed. [Take them] out of the Fire.' I will go and do so."

The Prophet ﷺ added, "I then return for a fourth time and praise Him similarly and fall down in prostration before Him. It will be said, 'O Muhammad, raise your head and speak, for you will be listened to; and ask, for you will be granted [your request]: and intercede, for your intercession will be accepted.' I will say, 'O Lord, allow me to intercede for whoever said, 'None has the right to be worshiped except Allah.' Then Allah will say, 'By my Power, and my Majesty, and by My Supremacy, and by My Greatness, I will take out of Hell whoever said: 'None has the right to be worshipped except Allah.'"[1]

[1] *Ṣaḥīḥ al-Bukhārī*, no. 7510.

104

Mufti Menk said "When we ask the Almighty for something, we should do so with trust and certainty that He will answer it. Never should we supplicate with a lazy mind and distracted heart. Ask wholeheartedly. Keep asking. Be patient and don't give up. Keep your heart calm. Attach it to your Creator. Ignore all the noise. The day you walk in Paradise is when every hardship will make sense. Hopelessness is a great sin. It's often the result of ignorance of the greatness of the Almighty. One should never give in to despair. Even in the worst-case scenario, there's a glimmer of hope in the heart. Always remember His Infinite Mercy. He will never turn anyone away.

If you want positive change, check your actions and what you're doing about them. There's no way you can expect change by sitting around and blaming others or the Almighty. Think of death often; the moment you're alone in your grave with only your deeds. It would be too late to wish if only you had done more. What are the same things you've been doing, over and over, that have made you stuck in a rut? Start changing them. If the Almighty has chosen to guide you, be thankful. Remember, He guides whom He wills and it's His Mercy that has enveloped you. Thank Him. Don't look down on those who have deviated from His path. He can change their situation any time!"[1]

Nouman Ali Khan discussed this idea of change and what it means when we forget to change. Allah ﷻ granted you a way to remember and whoever deliberately ignores it will have a great burden on the Day of Judgement. Would you carry a burden now or on the Day of Judgement? By carrying Allah's ﷻ word, life becomes easier and

[1] Mufti Menk, Motivational Moments II.

lighter. Whoever purposely ignores Allah ﷻ, there is no doubt this person has a life of *ḍank*—every part of their life is affected, with what? *Ḍank* is the feeling of having a stuffed nose when you cannot breathe; or when you feel stuffed; or when you fill a pillow with material—the idea of being full, filled and blocked.

This internal state causes weakness physically and emotionally, and will make you lose your clear intellectual reasoning. We must follow the commandments of Allah ﷻ. Not listening and ignoring the permissible and the impermissible is just like telling the doctor, "Don't finish your sentence doctor, I don't want to deal with that"; or it is like saying "Do not tell me when the exam is because then I have to start studying for it." The moment Allah ﷻ put us on earth, we are responsible. We are worthy of being asked. We will be asked. We are not roaming freely.

105

Ibn ʿUmar ﷺ said: "I was with the Messenger of Allah ﷺ and a man from among the Anṣār came to him and greeted the Prophet ﷺ with salām. Then he said: 'O Messenger of Allah, which of the believers is wisest and most decisive and strong willed?' He said: 'The one who remembers death often and is best in preparing for it. Those are the wisest! They win the honor of this life and the next.'[1]

The reason behind laziness and procrastination in performing righteous deeds and working for the Hereafter is forgetting about death and the fact that it comes suddenly. Al-Daqqāq رحمه الله, one of our pious predecessors, said: "The one who remembers death often is rewarded with three things:

1. Hastening to repent,

2. Contentment of heart, such that the loss of any form of this worldly life will not dishearten the person, and

3. Energy and zeal for worship.

And whoever forgets death is punished with three things:

1. Delaying repentance,

2. Not being content with what suffices them, and

3. Laziness in worship"

"The measure of divine grace the human receives towards dealing with events is directly proportional to how much they uphold

---

[1] Recorded by Ibn Mājah and classed as authentic by al-Albānī and other scholars of hadith.

commandments; if they are thorough in enacting commandments in both an outward and inward manner, they receive comparable grace both outwardly and inwardly. If they however uphold commandments in a superficial manner neglecting their actuality and inward requirements, they only receive outward grace correspondingly and their share of inward grace is limited. If one were to ask what is this inward divine grace? It is the tranquility, assurance, and the removal of worry, unrest, and fright that the heart will be gifted at times of adversity."[1]

---

[1] Ibn al-Qayyim, *al-Fawā'id*.

106

Imagine that you're shopping with someone you love. No, not just someone you love. Someone you dearly love. Now suppose that this person picks out a gift for you in a particular color and style. How would you feel about that gift? Chances are you'll cherish it simply because of who gave it to you. The fact that Allah ﷻ has chosen you in His infinite wisdom and mercy for this particular task, trial, storm, or blessing, says a lot. We must cherish whatever comes from Allah ﷻ because everything comes with extreme love and care towards us from Allah ﷻ. Allah ﷻ crafted your life and put you through each of the experiences for your benefit. Every one of the good and the bad experiences are there to get you on the road. Which road is that?

Guide us to the Straight Path. [The Quran, 1:6]

The religion of Allah ﷻ is law and wisdom. Sometimes the wisdom behind the laws or events in our lives is easily understandable and at other times it is not so easy. Everything that happens to you cannot always be understood directly. The wisdom behind events is always there, but you may not have access to it. Allah ﷻ sometimes will only tell you the command of doing something, and you have to trust Him. He has His own wisdom and knows the benefits, but He will not open all doors for you because He wants to see how much you are willing to trust Him. This idea started with shaytan. Prostrating to Adam ﷺ made no sense, but the law was there in the form of a command from Allah ﷻ. Just because you do not see the wisdom, it does not mean that Allah ﷻ has stopped being loving or caring. That is enough comfort.

Imam 'Alī ؓ used to say the people are sleeping. This message came to wake people up. People get annoyed when they are deep asleep and want to stay asleep and you try to wake them up, but you have to do it when there is a fire in the house. This teaching is so powerful, it is what gives us our dignity and identity. When we let go of this Book, we become nothing, we have nothing. So we cannot afford to loosen our grip on this Book.

This reminds us not to bend when things are tough, and the people who hold on to good will have a great reward. Allah ﷻ does not need us, this Book is worthy of being held on to and those who do not, they are not worthy of it. You are holding onto a tree in a flood whose roots are deep [the Quran], and you are kept alive by it. Everyone else is being washed away. And you will never find any place to hide or be safe other than in this Book, in His words.

107

The Prophet ﷺ said: "There are four qualities, whoever is given them has truly been given the best in this world and the next. They are a grateful heart [that is thankful to Allah ﷻ], a remembering tongue [that mentions Allah ﷻ often], an enduring body [to persevere through the trials which Allah ﷻ may send], and a faithful wife [who does not cheat him of her body or his wealth]."

The Prophet ﷺ told Muʿādh ﷺ: "By Allah [ﷻ], I love you, so do not forget to say at the end of every ṣalāh, 'O Allah [ﷻ], help me to remember You and to give thanks to You and to worship You well.'"[1]

The Prophet ﷺ said, "No blessing is bestowed on a slave, and he realizes that it is from Allah [ﷻ], but that the reward of giving gratitude for it is written for him. Never does Allah [ﷻ] know the regret of His slave for a wrong action he has committed, but that Allah [ﷻ] forgives his wrong action before the slave seeks forgiveness. No man buys a garment with his own money then puts it on and thanks Allah [ﷻ], but Allah [ﷻ] will have forgiven him all his wrong action before the garment reaches his knees."

"The mention of God Almighty smoothens what is rough, eases what is difficult and lightens what is heavy. As soon as God Almighty is mentioned, every rough [road] is smoothed, every difficulty eased, every burden lightened, every hardship removed, every woe lifted. The remembrance of God is the ease that follows difficulty, the relief that follows hardship, care, and woe. And this is [further] explained by [what follows]. The remembrance of God Almighty alleviates fear

---

[1] Aḥmad and al-Tirmidhī.

from the heart and has the wondrous effect of bringing about security. For someone who is frightened and seized by fear, there is nothing more beneficial than to mention God Almighty. And in proportion to his remembrance, he will find security, even in the thing that had [previously] caused him fear. The heedless man may be completely safe yet afraid, and all the safety he has will only increase his fear. Anyone with the least sense has experienced both this and that. God is the One from whom we seek aid."[1]

[1] Ibn al-Qayyim, *The Invocation of God*, p. 99.

108

> ... but it is best to be [beautifully] patient: from God alone I
> seek help to bear what you are saying. [The Quran, 12:18]

Nouman Ali Khan explained, "Why is the patience of Yaʿqūb ﷺ
beautiful? Beautiful because whatever happens, happens by Allah's
will ﷻ only and I don't get to question it. The One I resigned it to
[Allah ﷻ], is much wiser, fair, loving, and knowledgeable. Knowing
this, the right kind of patience leads to beautiful things. Our faith is
attacked by emotions, and what makes you beautiful is the faith you
have in your heart. Sometimes to protect our faith means to control
your emotions, because if your faith is gone, all is gone then.

Yaʿqūb ﷺ is telling himself something: he doesn't see anything
beautiful now but he has a promise from Allah ﷻ and it is a beautiful
promise; even though reality may be ugly, Allah's ﷻ words will help
me carry through the hardness, I won't lose hope in Allah ﷻ or have a
bad opinion of Allah ﷻ. From this one can deduce the opposite as
well, there must also be ugly patience with which resentment,
bitterness, anger, saying things under your breath, negative thoughts,
are built and takes the light away from your heart. You may be patient,
but it is not beautiful. No pain goes away because of patience; it means
I will have patience to preserve something beautiful (the light in your
heart, your faith) and doing that is painful but worth it a million times
over.

When you are being patient, Allah ﷻ sees the beauty in what you do—
Allah ﷻ seeing it as beautiful is good enough. When you exhibit
patience, it is the highest form of obedience to Allah ﷻ. Nothing in
my life is more beautiful than obeying Allah ﷻ. When we exhibit

patience, it may be that no one on earth is happy and you may not be happy but knowing Allah ﷻ is happy, that is the most beautiful thing. Sometimes you go through an experience and when it finishes you look back and think how Allah ﷻ got you through it and say wow that was a beautiful plan from Allah ﷻ.

Ya'qūb ﷺ knows Allah ﷻ so well, he knows that everything Allah ﷻ does is beautiful, even before seeing the end of the matter. Patience is a timeless thing—situations come and go but what doesn't go is patience. We have to remind ourselves (even a prophet had to) and say it out loud that patience is beautiful. You have to have self-talk. Whether what you want occurs or not, beautiful patience should never go away, and His plan always has wisdom and is taking care of His slaves better than anyone ever can. Say to yourself: whatever I'm going through Allah ﷻ knows about it and His planning for me is full of wisdom and I trust His plan more than I trust my desires—Allah ﷻ knows better. What you get and lose is a small part of this journey of life."

109

Allah ﷻ selected you because you are the right one, and as a result, Allah ﷻ will complete His favor on you. You are the right one to be pushed around, to be thrown in jail or in a well, or to be tempted. Your goodness can only come out in these moments, so we have to make the most of them. These are part of Allah ﷻ completing His favor upon you.

Allah ﷻ put a quality inside of believers to overcome the most powerful urges due to their love of Him. Without Allah's ﷻ mercy we cannot do it. Because you were good to Allah ﷻ, He will give you the strength to walk away from darkness. This comes as an act of love and care from Allah ﷻ, and it is a special type of mercy. The formula from Allah ﷻ is show Me your effort, I will give you the result.[1]

Desires and emotions are like flood waters that want to destroy a city, but *taqwā* [God-consciousness] comes and puts gates allowing water to go in certain channels, and when released from the proper channels, farms will be irrigated, people will drink and so forth, while if the gates are just opened then the city will be destroyed [your soul]. Your life will be blessed if you have *taqwā*. If you cannot win the battle inside, you cannot win the battle outside. If you have these two, then you will be a *muḥsin* which is the highest state of a believer.

You are a creature of hope. *Ṣabr* and *taqwā* often make you feel like you missed out, but Allah ﷻ says you never missed out and I will reward you. When Allah ﷻ wants someone to go through a certain trial then the easiest solutions become impossible, but when Allah ﷻ

[1] Bayyinah TV, Ramadan Gems.

wants to bring relief, the most impossible solutions become possible. In both hard and ease we have to remember the perfection of Allah ﷻ . Think about how great Allah ﷻ is, do not think about how big your sins or problems are.

The Quran has an explanation for everything you asked for, every issue and concern, every time you needed guidance and were stuck not knowing what to do, every time you could not conquer your fear or lost hope or were hurt by others. You came to this revelation with questions about you and the world inside you. Allah ﷻ helps you separate the different components of a situation: the role of the Devil, role of culture, your own bias.

The Quran is a way of looking at reality. It gives you a core way of thinking that will deal with a million issues. It will make you understand everything universally. Whoever even with low faith opens this book will be shown guidance and how much Allah ﷻ loves them. Nothing will bring you peace like the Quran. Allah ﷻ gave the worst of people the Quran who rejected it so what will Allah ﷻ do for those who seek it?

110

And your Lord inspired the bees: "Make your homes in the mountains, the trees, and in what people construct, and feed from the flower of any fruit you please and follow the ways your Lord has made easy for you." From their bellies comes forth liquid of varying colors, in which there is healing for people. Surely in this is a sign for those who reflect." [The Quran, 16:68-69]

"While excavating Egypt's famous pyramids, archaeologists have found pots of honey in an ancient tomb. The honey, dating back approximately 3,000 years, is the world's oldest sample—and still perfectly edible."[1]

"Think about the bees that made this honey. Think about the flowers they must have visited. Beautiful, colorful, fragrant flowers that have, since then, shriveled up and faded away. The bees, by following the inspiration from their Lord and working hard, took that which was temporary and transformed it into that which endures. Think of the flower as this *dunyā* and the choices it presents and think of the honey as good deeds that endure into the *ākhirah*. If we follow the commands of our Lord and work hard, together we can take just what we need from a fading world and transform it into good deeds that are everlasting."[2]

[1] National Geographic.
[2] A. Siddiqui's reflection.

Whatever you have will end, but whatever Allah has is everlasting. And We will certainly reward the steadfast according to the best of their deeds. [The Quran, 16:96]

لَا تَقْنَطُوا مِنْ رَحْمَةِ اللَّهِ ۚ إِنَّ اللَّهَ يَغْفِرُ الذُّنُوبَ جَمِيعًا

Do no despair of Allah's mercy, for indeed Allah forgives all sins.

This page intentionally left blank.

Journey 2

The Mercy of the Most Merciful, Allah ﷻ

The doors of the mercy of Allah ﷻ are only a door frame, there is no door. They are wide open for you to enter them. There is nothing so large that it does not fit in these doors.

Seeking Allah's ﷻ forgiveness is a door that knocks on the door of repentance and on the doors of sustenance and on the doors of mercy. Seeking forgiveness opens all these doors, for Allah ﷻ said:

> Ask forgiveness of your Lord: He is ever forgiving, [The Quran, 71:10]

> He will send down abundant rain from the sky for you; [The Quran, 71:11]

Is that it? No,

> He will give you wealth and offspring; [The Quran, 71:12]

That it? No,

> He will provide you with gardens, [The Quran, 71:12]

Is that it? No,

> And rivers. [The Quran, 71:12]

No servant of Allah ﷻ seeks sincere forgiveness other than Allah ﷻ grants them freedom from each one of their problems and a way out of every worry.

III

This righteous person beseeches and supplicates to Allah ﷻ through this door of mercy. Saying, "O Allah ﷻ, you say 'But whoever repents after his wrongdoing and reforms indeed, Allah will turn to him in forgiveness, indeed Allah is forgiving and merciful.' And here I have repented of my wrongdoing so have mercy on me." He beseeches Allah ﷻ with this.

Then continues... and if I am not worthy of it you said, "and He is ever merciful to the believers" and I am a believer so have mercy on me. If I am not worthy of it you said, "My mercy encompasses all things" and I am a thing so have mercy on me. And if I am not worthy of it then there's no calamity greater than mine. The mercy that encompasses all things does not encompass me—this surely is calamitous.

Now I say as you taught us, "Indeed we belong to Allah and indeed to Him we will return" and You say, "Those who when afflicted with calamity say, 'Indeed, we belong to Allah and indeed to Him we will return,' those are the ones upon whom are blessings from their Lord and mercy," hence bestow your mercy on me

He beseeches Allah ﷻ by all means.

112

Omar Suleiman said: "There is a very beautiful explanation for this verse, from a spiritual perspective by Imam al-Ḥasan al-Baṣrī رَحِمَهُاللّٰه, as well as from the great explainer (*mufassir*) of the Quran Mujāhid رَحِمَهُاللّٰه who said that Allah جَلَّ loves those who repent, i.e., those who do not insist upon sin and do not return to the same sin. They said those who do not engage in or those who do not insist upon committing those particular sins, so in other words they are insisting on returning to Allah جَلَّ.

Even if they do commit those sins at times; they insist upon returning to Allah جَلَّ. And the second explanation they gave was, they do not repeat the same sins over and over again as that would show disregard of Allah جَلَّ, that would show that they were not taking their repentance (*tawbah*) seriously, and that would show that they had not learnt this lesson.

There is something important to understand here, Allah جَلَّ loves us for trying, for being engaged in a state of purification. Allah جَلَّ loves us for repenting but where is it that we fall short? Those of us who repent sincerely for a sin and insist we will not return to that sin, yet still do so, that does not disqualify us from the love of Allah جَلَّ, nor does it open all the previous times we committed that sin nor does it nullify our previous repentance for that sin. But the type of insistence and returning to sin that could cause us to fall out of the love of Allah جَلَّ, out of this journey of attaining His love, is when we insist upon those sins and disregard the sight of Allah جَلَّ and disregard the pursuit of Allah جَلَّ by returning to those sins. So, there is a difference between falling short again, becoming weak again after we sincerely repent and not being sincere in our repentance or in our pursuit of purification in the first place."[1]

---

[1] Omar Suleiman, *Allah Loves*, pp. 31-32.

II3

'Abdullāh ibn Mas'ūd ﷺ related to us: "A believer sees his sins as if he were sitting under a mountain that he is afraid may fall on him; whereas the wicked person considers his sins as flies passing over his nose and he just drives them away like this."[1]

Al-Junayd, رحمه الله said, "If a man worships Allah for one thousand years, and then he turns away from him for one moment, then what he missed in this moment is more than what he gained in the one thousand years of worship."

Ibn al-Jawzī رحمه الله said, "One day I said in a sermon: 'O youth! You are like a person travelling in the desert while possessing priceless jewels that he intends to sell in the land of reward, so beware of falling into the trap of your treacherous desire so you do not end up selling what you have for less than what it is worth. Otherwise, when you reach your destination and see those who made great profits, you will cry for your loss and say, 'Oh how great is my regret over what I neglected in regard to Allah.' However, regret shall never restore what has been missed."[2]

---

[1] *Ṣaḥīḥ al-Bukhārī*, no. 6308.
[2] Ibn al-Jawzī, *Awakening from the Sleep of Heedlessness*.

114

A Message of Hope [1]

> Tell them, [O Prophet], "My servants who have committed excesses against themselves, do not despair of Allah's Mercy. Surely Allah forgives all sins. He is Most Forgiving, Most Merciful." [The Quran, 39:53]

To address such a thing to the common men does not mean that Allah ﷻ forgives all sins without repentance, no! Allah ﷻ Himself has explained in the following verses that sins are forgiven only when the sinner turns to Allah's ﷻ worship and service and adopts obedience to the message sent down by Him. The purpose of this verse is to instill a sense of hope in the heart of those sinners who might feel overwhelmed with fear and regret.

It's a message of hope from the Most Merciful and Most Kind. As a matter of fact, it's a message for those people who had committed mortal sins like murder, adultery, theft, robbery, and so forth in the days of ignorance, and had despaired whether they would ever be forgiven. To those sinners, and to all who commit similar or lesser type of sins, it has been said: "Do not despair of Allah's mercy: whatever you might have done in the past, if you sincerely turn to your Lord's obedience, you will be forgiven every sin." Turn to Allah ﷻ, The Most Merciful, with a sincere repentance knowing that He will, undoubtedly, accept you back, and elevate your rank merely as a result of your sincere repentance!

[1] Semir Nour.

115

Habib Umar bin Hafiz, May Allah ﷻ reward him, was asked, "Many young people complain that it is difficult for them to leave certain acts of disobedience. When they do manage to repent, they often fall into the same sin again. How are they able to repent sincerely?

Do not deem yourself incapable of repenting even if you keep committing the sin a hundred times a day. Do not forget that you have Allah ﷻ, Who is completely aware of you. As long as you repent to Him sincerely, He will see this, even if you keep repeating the same sin. He will rid you of this disobedience in due course, according to your sincerity. The Prophet ﷺ said, 'By Him in whose hand is my soul, if you did not sin, Allah would replace you with people who would sin and then seek forgiveness from Allah and He would forgive them.'"

You must never cut your connection to Him. Never believe what the Devil, your enemy, tells you. Do not say to yourself, "There is no hope for me and that I will never be able to stop doing this." No! This is a ploy which your lower self and the Devil uses to cut you off from Allah ﷻ. Go back to Him in a state of remorse and humility, and say, "O Lord, help me." If you fall into it again, return to Allah ﷻ with remorse once again, repent and resolve never to do it again. When Allah ﷻ witnesses your sincerity and persistence, He will have mercy on you. He will strengthen you and save you from this act of disobedience, whenever He wishes.

116

Ibn al-Jawzī رحمه الله wrote, "Does the one who keeps delaying and postponing his repentance think that his desires will ever abate? No indeed, for what keeps him from repenting today shall accompany him tomorrow and the day after; it is because with the passage of days it only becomes stronger and more deep-rooted within him. This is evident because 'As the Son of Adam becomes old, two of his qualities grow old with him; his love of wealth and his hope of living longer.'[1]

The only way to find comfort in this life is by regarding it as a means to an end, not by intimately befriending it. When the pious and judicious realized the flaws and shortcomings of this life, they did not waste another moment of their life in idle play. And so, their self-discipline led them to spacious gardens and in the end, they settled in the paradise of affability [with Allah] in the shade of [seeking the Hereafter].

O you who prefers the cemetery of sleep over the gardens of the pious, the path of joining ties with your Lord does not entail exhaustion; because exhaustion is only felt by those whose hearts still contain desires. Indeed, the night is not dark for Layla[2] as it is for others.

---

[1] Reported by Bukhārī (6421) and Muslim (1049).

[2] A reference to the story of Layla and Qays. When they were separated from each other Qays spent his days composing poetry praising Layla and so the night was for them a moment where both remembered each other.

The deviated one is astray from the right path; fly you instead with the wings of hope and fear, leaving the nest of apathy behind you; stand firmly on the Right Path, and work hard."[1]

"Nobody has a perfect past. We all sin. So don't let that come between you and the Almighty. He is waiting to forgive. He loves it when you ask and repent and depend on Him. That's our Lord. Our Creator! Don't wait to repent. Don't listen to the whispering of Satan. Don't let your trickle of sin become an ocean of regret. That's foolish because the Almighty is always there to welcome you back on His Path. You only have to connect with Him. Ask Him. Sincerely."[2]

[1] Ibn al-Jawzī, *Seeds of Admonishment and Reform*, p. 180.
[2] Mufti Menk, Motivational Moments II.

117

The Prophet ﷺ said: "When a servant desires to commit a sin, nothing is recorded against him. If he then leaves that sin for the sake of Allah, one good deed is recorded for him, if he commits that sin, one sin is recorded for him, if he leaves that sin, but not for the sake of Allah, no sin or reward is recorded for him."[1]

Ibn Taymiyyah رحمه الله wrote: "So Yūsuf رحمه الله had a desire which he abandoned for the sake of Allah and this is why Allah turned him away from evil and indecency by virtue of his sincerity. Hence, this turning away occurs when the cause for committing sin is present, i.e., desire, yet contending with this is one's sincerity to Allah. So, Yūsuf رحمه الله did nothing except good deeds for which he would be rewarded for."

> Those who are aware of God think of Him when Satan prompts them to do something and immediately, they can see [straight]; The followers of devils are led relentlessly into error by them and cannot stop. [The Quran, 7:201-202]

---

[1] Ṣaḥīḥ Muslim, no. 130.

118

The Prophet ﷺ said, "Allah, Blessed is He and Most High, said: 'O son of Adam! Verily as long as you called upon Me and hoped in Me, I forgave you, despite whatever may have occurred from you, and I did not mind. O son of Adam! Were your sins to reach the clouds of the sky, then you sought forgiveness from Me, I would forgive you, and I would not mind. So, son of Adam! If you came to me with sins nearly as great as the earth, and then you met Me not associating anything with Me, I would come to you with forgiveness nearly as great as it.'"[1]

Abū Mūsā reported Allah's Messenger ﷺ as saying, "Allah, the Exalted and Glorious, stretches out His Hand during the night so that the people may repent for the fault committed from dawn till dusk and He stretches out His Hand during the day so that the people may repent for the fault committed from dusk to dawn. [He will continue accepting repentance until] before the sun rises in the west [i.e., until the Day of Judgment]."[2]

Qatādah said, "The Holy Quran points out the illness and its cure. Your illnesses are sins, and your cure is asking for forgiveness."

> Your Lord says, 'Call on Me and I will answer you; those who are too proud to serve Me will enter Hell humiliated.' [The Quran, 40:60]

---

[1] Al-Tirmidhī, no. 3540.
[2] Ṣaḥīḥ Muslim, no. 2759a, b.

119

A poet said[1]

And surely, I call upon Allah ﷻ and seek His Pardon
And I know that Allah ﷻ pardons and forgives
And even if the people commit great sins
Their sins compared to the Mercy of Allah ﷻ are small

Al-Fudhayl ibn 'Iyād saw people glorifying Allah ﷻ and crying while calling upon Him. So, Al-Fudhayl asked those with him, "If these people were to beg a man in this manner for a *dāniq* [1/6 of a dirham, equivalent to around a penny] would the man that they are begging turn them away?" They said, "By Allah ﷻ, he would not turn them away!" Al-Fudhayl said, "It is easier for Allah ﷻ to grant forgiveness than it is for a man to give a beggar a *dāniq*."

Do not be miserly with your prostrations to Allah ﷻ. You were created from an insignificant drop, but when man puts his head down on the ground in prostration to Allah ﷻ, then he is greater than all creation. Allah ﷻ will raise you from the depths of darknesses and pull you out.

[1] Narrated by Shaykh Ahson Syed.

120

I said: "My sins are so many..."

Allah ﷻ said: "And who can forgive sins except Allah?" [The Quran, 3:135]

I said: "Do not abandon me..."

Allah ﷻ said: "So, remember me, I will remember you." [The Quran, 2:15]

I said: "I'm facing so many difficulties..."

Allah ﷻ said: "And whoever fears Allah, He will make for him a way out." [The Quran, 65:2]

I said: "I have many of aspirations..."

Allah ﷻ said: "Call upon Me, I will respond to you." [The Quran: 40:60]

We have Allah ﷻ, our loving Nurturer and Provider Who wants to listen to us. He wants to hear your dua. Regarding the Companions of the Cave Allah ﷻ says:

> Then We woke them so that We could make clear which of the two parties was better able to work out how long they had been there. [The Quran, 18:12]

Nouman Ali Khan commented regarding this, "Allah ﷻ places more value on their internal conversation, which may seem trivial at first glance, as His demonstration of closeness to Him. In comparison to them being a miracle or a powerful reminder of resurrection or a great inspiration to the Ummah of Muhammad ﷺ, the rationale for their resurrection that is given priority is that Allah ﷻ wants to hear their back and forth and the conversation that happens. Allah ﷻ is their loving friend who wants to observe the spectacle of their arguments and conversations. Before He tells us that He raised them for anyone else's benefit He tells us He raised them for His pleasure and His own joy. These young men in their lonely quest for the cave turned to Allah ﷻ alone in prayer. Allah ﷻ responded directly to them when no one else could. His love for them is manifest not just how He put them to sleep but His interest in their conversation (of how many days they slept). No academic, king or historian has ever been closer to the people."[1]

Similarly, Allah ﷻ says:

"Mūsā, what is that in your right hand?" [The Quran, 20:17]

Mūsā ﷺ him replies:

"It is my staff,' he said, "I lean on it; restrain my sheep with it; I also have other uses for it." [The Quran, 20:18]

Allah ﷻ, despite knowing it is a staff, still asks and wants to hear His servant's voice and reply. Although Allah ﷻ knows what is bothering you and what your problems are, He wants you to talk to Him, through the believer's most powerful weapon: dua. Despite all the noise the temporary world makes, stay focused on Allah ﷻ. Everything else will fall into place. "What's with Allah ﷻ lasts." if what

---

[1] Bayyinah TV, Surat al-Kahf Deeper Look.

is with Allah ﷻ lasts after we have departed this world, then what is with Him will maintain us through it!

121

And to lose hope in the One who grants you higher ranks after falling then repenting is the greatest calamity. Allah's ﷻ infinite mercy encompasses us even in times we are weak and sinful. May Allah ﷻ forgive us for our shortcomings. Return to Allah even if you have sinned a million times.[1]

"Never lose hope in His Mercy. Never believe that you're too far gone to ask for forgiveness. He knows your struggle. He created you!"[2]

Omar Suleiman, may Allah ﷻ reward him, wrote, "Repentance means we actually get closer to Allah ﷻ than we were before we committed the sin, we become more beloved to Him than before. This is why it's not unjust that Allah ﷻ created us and gave us the free will to sin, because the degree that He guarantees us for repenting after committing a sin is even greater than that of His sinless creatures, the angels, who have no free will. Penitent human beings ascend even beyond the angels in rank.

Ibn al-Qayyim رحمه الله puts these ideas together and gives us the example of two Prophets. He explained that the Devil was delighted when he saw that he had caused Adam's عليه السلام fall. What he didn't realize was that when a diver goes into the ocean, he collects pearls at the bottom, and he rises back up again. Adam عليه السلام was better after his *tawbah* even though he had to come down to this earth. His rank with Allah ﷻ was higher after his repentance than when he was in Paradise. In the same way Yūnus عليه السلام was better after he was swallowed by the whale than he was before it happened. That is why Allah ﷻ said, "His

[1] Ibn Abi Muhammad.
[2] Mufti Menk, Motivational Moments Part II.

Lord chose him and made him from the righteous" after he was swallowed by the whale.

There is no such thing as a sin that can permanently disqualify you from the love of Allah ﷻ if you repent afterwards and use that to propel yourself towards Him."[1]

Mufti Menk said, "Never feel like the Almighty is getting tired of you. So even if you've been sinning repeatedly, repent. He loves it when you repent."[2]

---

[1] Omar Sulieman, *Allah Loves*, p. 11.
[2] Mufti Menk, Motivational Moments Part II.

122

Repentance to the oft forgiving One, Allah ﷻ, revives our souls from the dead and gives life to us.

The aching breaths of Adam ﷺ started burning him when [Allah ﷻ said],

> Adam disobeyed [The Quran, 21:121]

and would have overcome him had he not been saved by the water of:

> He accepted his repentance. [The Quran, 2:37][1]

Here is an account of the last man to enter Paradise which demonstrates the sweetness and vastness of Allah's ﷻ mercy towards someone who was in the fire:

This last man says, after being taken out of Hell, "Allah has given me something He has not given to any one of those in earlier or later times." Then a tree would be raised up for him and he will say, "O my Lord, bring me near this tree so that I may take shelter in its shade and drink of its water." Allah, the Exalted and Great, would say, "O son of Adam, if I grant you this, you will ask Me for something else." He would say, "No, my Lord!" And he would promise Him that he would not ask for anything else. His Lord would excuse him because He sees what he cannot help desiring; so He would bring him near it, and he would take shelter in its shade and drink of its water.

---

[1] Ibn al-Jawzī, *Seeds of Admonishment and Reform*, p. 35.

Afterwards a tree more beautiful than the first would be raised up before him and he would say: "O my Lord! bring me near this tree in order that I may drink of its water and take shelter in its shade and I shall not ask Thee for anything else." He [Allah ﷻ] would say, "O son of Adam, if I bring you near it you may ask me for something else." He would promise Him that he would not ask for anything else. Then a tree would be raised up for him at the gate of Paradise, more beautiful than the first two. He would say: "O my Lord! bring me near this [tree] so that I may enjoy its shade and drink from its water. I shall not ask You for anything else."

His Lord would excuse him for He sees something the temptation of which he could not resist. He [Allah] would bring him near to it, and when He would bring him near it he would hear the voices of the inhabitants of the Paradise. He would say, "O my Lord! admit me to it." He (Allah) would say, "O son of Adam, what will bring an end to your requests to Me? Will it please you if I give you the whole world and a like one along with it?"[1] Then,

"The Prophet ﷺ would also laugh whenever he would share narrations about Allah's ﷻ infinite mercy, such as the narration of the last man who will enter Paradise. This man will think that Allah ﷻ is mocking him because he does not fathom the scope of Allah's ﷻ mercy and generosity. The Prophet ﷺ laughed when relating this narration, and said: "Allah ﷻ laughs at that man when the man said, 'O Allah (ﷻ) are you making fun of me? And you are the Lord of the world?' It should be noted that his laugh was not audible, but it was clearly distinct from his customary smile, as his back teeth would be visible."[2]

---

[1] Ṣaḥīḥ Muslim, no. 187.

[2] Omar Suleiman, *Meeting Muhammad* ﷺ, p. 14.

"The leniency of Allah ﷻ toward His slaves is pre-eternal. As the child is born, He sparks for him a river of milk coming out from the springs of his mother's breast and implanted instinctual love towards him into the hearts of his parents until He overwhelms them with His grace. Yet, after this child grows up and becomes aware of the One Who bestowed all these graces upon him, he utilizes all these graces in disobeying Allah ﷻ. As the poet have said:

A person spends his nights wearing the robe of impiety,
Nevertheless Allah covers him with the shelter of
His forbearance without knowing so.

The son of Adam rushes to issue forth a challenge [i.e., start involving in acts of disobedience]! But for whose interest? And against whom? To get to where? And who are you in the first place to proclaim a challenge?

O you! Allah ﷻ has bestowed upon you a mercy incomparable to any other mercy; when you repent from your sins, He orders his angels to overlook what he recorded against you, and when He judges you He covers your shortcomings so that others do not see the yellowness of your skin caused by your shame. O you whose innate nature is that of purity, beware of debasing yourself with the filth of sins. Lift up the tails of piety above the trash of self-desires and beware of the sprays of mistakes so it does not touch your pure garments. And know that the fountain of your eyes shall wash off the dirt staining your heart. It is amazing how the Possessor of the Creation [i.e., Allah ﷻ] asks His slaves to drop a tear though He created the seven oceans."[1]

---

[1] Ibn al-Jawzī, *Seeds of Admonishment and Reform*, pp. 134-138.

123

In Sūrat al-Fātiḥah, after stating that Allah ﷻ is the Lord of the worlds, that He is their sustainer and nurturer, the surah proceeds to show that this sustaining and nurturing is not done because Allah ﷻ is in need of the creation, but because of His mercy. Hence His Lordship is one of mercy and justice and not one of subjugation and oppression; He does not oppress his servants in the slightest, every punishment from Him arises from pure justice and every blessing arises from pure grace.

Through believing that Allah ﷻ is All-Merciful, the servant is encouraged to praise Allah ﷻ more. Just as Allah ﷻ has nurtured and sustained us in the best of ways, granting us blessings after blessings, so too should we nurture and cultivate ourselves and those who are placed in our care, upon mercy and justice, using those same blessings Allah ﷻ has bestowed on us. Just as Allah ﷻ is merciful, so too should we be merciful in nature and in deed,

The Prophet ﷺ said: "Al-Raḥmān shows mercy to the merciful. Have mercy on those who are on earth and the One who is above the heaven will have mercy on you."[1] The Prophet ﷺ also said, "Whoever is merciful, even when it comes to slaughtering a bird, Allah [ﷻ] will show him mercy on the Day of Judgment." From the names of Allah ﷻ al-Raḥmān and al-Raḥīm [the extremely loving and caring and the always loving and caring]. They both come from *raḥmah*. *Raḥm* is the belly [womb] of the mother. *Raḥmān* gave the name to *raḥm* [womb]. "A strange relationship is that of the baby and the mother. The mother suffers, gives all the food to the baby and as the baby grows, she suffers

---

[1] Al-Tirmidhī, no. 1924.

230

more, yet the love she has for the child only increases. The baby has no idea of this love and care. Allah ﷻ wanted to show us something through these names; He gives and gives unlimitedly, cares, loves, and protects, and we have no idea. We are enveloped in Allah's ﷻ care, protection, and mercy.

Raḥīm: someone who has a quality and even if it doesn't come out, it's there. It means someone who is always loving and caring. If Allah ﷻ only said *Raḥmān*, then it wouldn't be forever. Allah ﷻ wanted us to know His love, care and protection is coming right now and will always be there. He took care of our present and future. The present is mentioned first through *Raḥmān* because humans are first concerned with the present, but once satisfied, then move to thinking about the future where then Allah ﷻ mentions *Raḥīm*."[1]

[1] Bayyinah TV, Ramadan Gems.

124

O you who delays his repentance because of his deluded hope of a long life; tell me

For what Day was it postponed? [The Quran, 77:12]

You used to say, I will repent when my hair becomes gray [i.e., when I get old] and here they are, the months of summer [i.e., youth] have passed and gone and if the sword of your endeavors was of any use, your vain desires would have met their death under its sharp edge. Every day you lay down the basis of your repentance and returning to Allah 🕮, but you position this foundation on the edge of a precipice, because every time you get the heartfelt feeling to repent, the troops of your desires attack and overcome your intention of repentance.

Slaughter the throat of desire with the knife of firm resolve, because so long as desire remains alive, you are never safe from the relapses of an ever-changing heart [from good to evil]. Let the tears you shed in the darkness of the night be your intercessors for when you make mistakes. Indeed, the flint of the intercessor flames the sparks of success.

With the ink of your tears write your good expectation from He Who is capable of fulfilling them; do not be satisfied with your repentance without accompanying it with grief and sorrow similar to the grief of Prophet Ya'qūb 🕮 [when he lost Yūsuf 🕮] or the patience of Prophet Yūsuf 🕮 [over what he had gone through]; but if you cannot bear either of those, then at least accompany it with the humility of the brothers of Yūsuf 🕮 [when they said]:

and be charitable with us. [The Quran, 12:88]

O you who constantly makes mistakes, when will you prostrate the forehead of

and indeed, we have been sinners. [The Quran, 12:91]

When firm truthfulness and sincerity descends into the heart of the repenting slave, the King becomes pleased, and He writes off the written [bad deeds] and reveals to the earth: conceal the faults of my slave. Before you, there was a man who took a hundred lives, but then he repented and set forth [from his evil town to a good town] but death overtook him on the way. Thereupon, angels of mercy disputed with angels of punishment [as each side wanted to take this man's soul]. Allah ﷻ sent to them an angel to arbitrate between them, who said: measure the distance between the two towns, then Allah ﷻ commanded the town of evil to recede back further and the town of the good to come closer. When they measured the distances, they found the man closer to the town of the good, and thus he was forgiven.

Neither the judge nor the adversaries realize the wisdom of

thus we plan for Yūsuf, [The Quran, 12:30]

[Allah ﷻ pledges that] if a sinner repents sincerely, He will accept him and revive him and,

made for him light by which to walk among the people. [The Quran, 6:122]

O you who repent,

fulfill [all] contracts, [The Quran, 5:1]

and honor [your contract] with the One with Whom you made a contract, if you slip after having become upright, then return again to the house of Generosity [where] 'Allah [﷾] shall not tire [of forgiving you] until you are tired [of seeking forgiveness].'"[1]

Shaykh Semir Nour said, "Allah ﷻ instructed us all to hasten our individual return to Him. He wants us to come back to Him with a swift repentance—as close in time to the occurrence of the sin as possible. This is to prevent the heart from forming love and contentment to the sin—which is bound to happen over time, and with regular repetition of the sin. Hence a Muslim is commanded to wash his heart with a quick repentance. A genuine, sincere repentance that develops disgust and hatred towards that sin. Allah ﷻ promised to forgive all sins, for those who repent. However, He has also decreed, with His infinite Justice and Wisdom that anyone who develops love and contentment to sin, they shall be misguided by Allah ﷻ. Allah ﷻ will turn the heart of such individual away from guidance and away from any form of obedience and worship. Such individual shall find it extremely difficult to do anything righteous."

> This is because they intensely loved the life of this world and preferred it to the life in the Hereafter, and Allah does not show the Way of salvation to those people who are ungrateful! [The Quran, 16:107]

---

[1] Ibn al-Jawzī, *Seeds of Admonishment and Reform*, pp. 51-54.

125

I learned patience from a small boy...

Imam Fudhayl bin 'Iyāḍ ﷺ said, "I learned patience from a small boy. On my way to the masjid one day, I came across a woman beating her son at home. As he was yelling and screaming, he managed to open the door and flee. So, his mother locked the door on him. When I returned from the masjid, I found the boy, after having cried and wept, sleeping at the door of his home longing for his mother. So, his mother's heart softened, and she opened the door for him. Upon witnessing this, Fudhayl bin Iyad ﷺ cried until his beard became wet with tears, and then he said 'SubhanAllah! If only the servant was to be patient at the door of Allah ﷻ, Allah ﷻ would surely open it!'"[1]

Wonder at the infinite mercy of Allah ﷻ which has no limits or bounds. Shaykh Ibn 'Uthaymīn ﷺ said, "Sincere repentance is accepted no matter how grievous the sin."[2] He ﷺ also said, "Always keep in mind the fact that Allah wants you to be happy all the time, far from grief."[3]

Ibn al-Jawzī ﷺ said to this effect, "Indeed, it may be that sin be the cause of person's admission into Paradise. If a person redeems himself with sincerity, his soul which in the past used to incite him to commit sin will be transformed into a tranquil soul. When a repenting person converses with his faculties of sensibility and contemplation, they remind him of his previous sins and make him regret at his mounting audacity. Thereupon, the eyes that used to indulge in sin erupt with

[1] *Muṣannaf Ibn Abı Shaybah*, 6/22.
[2] *Fatāwa Nūr 'ala al-Darb.*
[3] *Sharḥ Bulūgh al-Marām*, 3/532-533.

tears of regret, and the repenting tongue repeats the words: I shall never return to sins ever after, and the functionary of bracing begins deploying hard workers to build up the edifice of his heart.

There, O sinner, whenever you are troubled by a matter, let your tears atone your affairs. O you who severed the connection to his Lord, return. O you who vowed to reject his Lord, repent. You were honored when Iblīs [Satan] was ordered to prostrate to you, whereas Iblīs was cast afar when he refused to do so. Yet I truly wonder at you! How could you, dispute that, make reconciliation with the Devil and boycott your Lord? How ruined you are, for your status in the Eyes of your Lord is greater than the status of the Night of Power [i.e., *Laylat al-Qadr*]."[1]

---

[1] Ibn al-Jawzī, *Seeds of Admonishment and Reform*, pp. 107-108.

126

Rush towards forgiveness from your Master. Forgiveness is especially attributed to Allah ﷻ. Allah ﷻ is teaching us that when you do something wrong, angering Allah ﷻ, He is still your caretaker, nurturer, you still have to run back towards Him. You must not delay doing good. Remove the bad with good. When you truly love someone, it is hard to face them when you have done wrong towards them. But Allah ﷻ is ready to receive you. The more we seek forgiveness, the more the sin is covered until, as the Quran describes it, it is "buried". Rush to cover your sins. Without forgiveness there is no Paradise.

> those who remember God and implore forgiveness for their sins if they do something shameful or wrong themselves—who forgives sins but God?—and who never knowingly persist in doing wrong. [The Quran, 3:135]

In other words, these shameful deeds will happen in one way or another for everyone; at some level. Humans are bound to slip; it is something expected. It is like peeling an onion, they peel layer by layer and remove their shameful deeds, never going back to them again. This is Allah's ﷻ way of saying as much as you are of the *muttaqīn* [those who have *taqwā*], you can still fall into error. As much as you try to protect yourself, you are still human and will make mistakes. This does not mean that Paradise is not prepared for you anymore.

Allah ﷻ, instead of saying that they ask for forgiveness once they wrong themselves, He says they first remember Him ﷻ, then they seek forgiveness. This piece in the middle is unexpected; "remembered Allah ﷻ". They either 1) remembered Allah ﷻ as an act of the heart 2) or mentioned Allah's ﷻ name.

It is required to remembering Allah ﷻ before asking for forgiveness. For a sinner, the heart goes away from Allah ﷻ—how and why? Because they forget certain things about Allah ﷻ [which shaytan wants them to], then the heart goes away from Allah ﷻ.

Someone who knows Allah ﷻ and His Names, will remember them. What is the name that captures all of His qualities? It is "Allah" ﷻ. It means they remembered Allah ﷻ for who He truly is. As a result of who Allah ﷻ is [which they lost sight of] they then ask for forgiveness.

You first fix your heart in regards to who Allah ﷻ is, then ask for forgiveness, because you have to know whom you are seeking forgiveness from.

Seeking forgiveness is also a matter of the heart. "For their sins (plural)": *dhanb* comes for *dhanab* which is the tail of an animal; a part of you that you are ashamed of. They sought Allah ﷻ to cover what is embarrassing to them and what brings them down. Darkness that comes down on us and the Devil says, "That's all you are, look at what you have, this is where you belong." These people recognized that Allah ﷻ gives new life every morning. Yesterday was a different life. Its shame, darkness, and guilt does not overshadow today or tomorrow and Allah ﷻ will cover it because it was another life. People will want to remind you, even keep you in yesterday, but with Allah ﷻ it is different.

Then Allah ﷻ puts a sentence in between a sentence which is an emotional statement. Allah says, "Then who will forgive mistakes if not Allah ﷻ?" Allah ﷻ is going further to touch the heart of His slave by saying: do you hear what I said? Who will cover your sins if not Allah ﷻ? Allah ﷻ is never one you can lose hope in. By placing this here, Allah ﷻ is giving us the reason to seek forgiveness: where will you turn, and whom will you turn to, if not Allah ﷻ?

Allah ﷻ has only done good to you. You remember Him as the one taking care of you, protecting you, watching over you. Imam al-Ālūsī رحمه الله says Allah ﷻ put this in the middle to remind us first of all how important it is to Allah ﷻ to tell you before He even finishes His sentence that you have nowhere to turn—"Come back to me come back to me!" And so that you never forget that whenever there is reason for forgiveness, Allah ﷻ forgives.

Ask forgiveness once and Allah ﷻ forgives all sins, great or small, old or new. Allah ﷻ covers even the things you have forgotten about. When Allah ﷻ covers them, it is as if they did not even take place. There is no place to hide, and no hope of finding refuge, for people who sins, except in Allah's ﷻ grace and mercy. Allah ﷻ, by placing this statement here, is giving the reader hope and reason for optimism. When the servant looks at this intense favor from Allah ﷻ, it encourages them further to turn back to Allah ﷻ. Allah ﷻ will banish the hopelessness and despair from our hearts. Allah ﷻ is saying when I forgive it is like a flood. Allah's ﷻ forgiveness is greater, no matter how great the sins are. Allah ﷻ decides to forgive you, even when people keep telling you that Allah ﷻ will not forgive you; Allah ﷻ is saying who do you think has the authority, power and right judgment to forgive if not Allah ﷻ?

Allah ﷻ describes the journey of those who have sinned and still want to go to heaven. They do not insist on sinning over and over again. They do not take advantage of His forgiveness. Ibn ʿAbbās ﷺ said, "Every sin that a slave keeps on doing is a major sin, and nothing is great if the slave repented from it." The Prophet ﷺ said, "Show love and care, you will be shown love and care. Cover others and you will be covered. Forgive others and you will be forgiven. Doom is headed towards those through whom good words pass like a cup without a bottom, and doom is for those who keep insisting on doing wrong."

They do not insist on their sin knowingly now that they know who Allah is. They have not insisted on sin, and they have been forgiven. Others say they do not insist because they know the ugly effect.[1]

[1] Bayyinah, Deeper Look Sūrat Āl 'Imrān.

127

Knowing Allah ﷻ is the most precious feeling in the universe. It brings life back to our heart and picks us up.

Nouman Ali Khan said, "Two names of Allah ﷻ: Near [Qarīb] and Responding [Mujīb]. We often have close relations and the closer they are we have more expectations, but they can fail to give us what we ask of them. They can be near but are not responding. Allah ﷻ is closer to us than anyone and He also responds. Mujīb: responds immediately. How to get closer to Allah ﷻ? Allah ﷻ sent the Quran. 'When my servants come to ask you [the ones who want to learn about Him] about Me, I am absolutely close.' Each one of us has different problems, so Allah ﷻ says He answers every dua. People forget about Allah ﷻ and do not listen to Allah ﷻ, but when in trouble or sick, they turn back to Allah ﷻ. Allah ﷻ could say where were you? Yet Allah ﷻ still helps them.

Who does He respond to? The one who calls. Allah ﷻ does not say "someone who is God-fearing", etc. Allah ﷻ is always close to us no matter where we run. When we get away from Allah ﷻ, shaytan says, "Allah ﷻ is away from you, why would Allah ﷻ listen to you?" etc.

Allah ﷻ says anyone who calls Him, He will answer immediately. Allah ﷻ says He knows the person by name, and they are special to Him. The more important someone is, the harder to get their time. Allah ﷻ says "whenever he calls Me." As if Allah ﷻ is waiting for your dua because He says WHEN you call not IF you call. His closeness and love keep Him waiting for you to turn back to him—He has already spoken to you, now it is your turn. Allah ﷻ says I will be Qarīb and Mujīb. Meaning, then at the very least, try to respond to Allah ﷻ.

Allah ﷻ acknowledges that we are slow and it is not immediate—"listen to my Quran [at least know what I am trying to say] and at least try to respond to Me. And you should have faith in Me." His advice is to make things easy for you as He loves you and cares about you, giving you the best advice. We have turns and twists in life, Allah ﷻ says, "if you respond to Me, I will make sure you stay on the right path." You and I have to ask with hope in Allah ﷻ. Have faith in Allah ﷻ. We have to acknowledge our weakness and submit to Allah ﷻ.

When people ask us for favors over and over again, they say what did you ever do for me? How much does Allah ﷻ do for us and how little we thank Him. Then we need something again and we do not even ask and yet Allah ﷻ grants us. Even when we disobey Allah ﷻ, Allah ﷻ does not forget us. However little you do or thank Allah ﷻ, He extremely appreciates it, even if it is small. Even though Allah ﷻ gave us what we have, He still appreciates it. Our deeds have shortcomings, and He will fill these shortcomings. Allah ﷻ appreciates the smallest good even when we do terrible crimes. He doesn't erase the good we have done and still appreciates and loves us."

128

You have a merciful Master who thinks about you and awaits your supplication, so you are never returned empty handed once you go to Him. Remember there is a mere doorway, no door, between you and the Lord of the Worlds.

Ibn al-Jawzī رحمه الله wrote, "Hasten to benefit from what remains! Let the delinquent collect what he has missed; let the one-eyed person be careful of stones thrown in his direction in case they hit his only sound eye. Do not underestimate the value of even a simple good deed. Your hearts have lost the way in the desolate land of vain desires so rise now on the feet of endeavor, pay no heed to the crowded road, and strive to make full effort, seeking whatever means are available to you; just as Yaʻqūb عليه السلام directed his sons,

> go and find out about Yūsuf and his brother and despair not of relief from Allah. [The Quran, 12: 87]

Take all means to recover what you have lost and do not despair of the Mercy of Allah ﷻ; indeed, many people have been healed though they were on the verge of ruin. How many opportunities have called out to you but you have missed out! Indeed, the mercy of Allah ﷻ is vast and encompassing. And take from this life only the bare necessities that you need in order to reach your final destination [i.e., the Hereafter]. Indeed, the demands of life and its vagaries can change one's purpose and alter one's course, causing the one walking on the path to Allah ﷻ to falter, but,

> whoever fears Allah He will make for him a way out. [The Quran, 65:2]

Therefore, whatever fate has decreed upon you in happiness or Calamity,

> so let there not be in your breast distress therefrom. [The Quran, 7: 2]

When Adam ﷺ and Eve ate from the forbidden tree, they found themselves encircled by calamitous dismay; they were hit by the rod of departure, banished from heaven and sent to earth. Nevertheless, it is the same One Who sent them down Who asks every night, 'Is there anyone asking Me so that I may grant him his request? Is there anyone asking My forgiveness, so that I may forgive him?' O you who has become cut off from the path of spiritual connection; will you not get back on track? Did you dedicate yourself to your Lord, or to everything else except Him?"[1]

---

[1] Ibn al-Jawzī, *Seeds of Admonishment and Reform*, pp. 211-215.

129

Ibn al-Jawzī رحمه الله said: "Beware of sins, for if they did not have any punishment other than feeling the shame of meeting your Lord while you carry these sins upon you, it would have been enough. The best moment of Ya'qūb عليه السلام was when he saw Yūsuf عليه السلام [after their separation] and the most difficult moment to the brothers of Yūsuf عليه السلام was when they met him [after they had wronged him].

If the heart was pure, it would be in a tumult when a sin was committed, but if the sin was repeated often then it would pass by the heart without being noticed or rejected. When the sin is alien to the heart, the heart feels a foreign presence that it finds discomfiting. But when the heart is used to the sin, the heart will become accustomed to it, and will accept it without a second thought. This is like the example of a person who wears a black garment, since he will not be concerned if he spills black on it."

"How did shaytan know that eating from the tree will get the clothes our father and mother removed in Paradise? As if it is a known fact, when someone disobeys Allah ﷻ, humiliation follows. Sins bring death to the heart and humiliation follows. In the words of the great scholar al-Ḥasan al-Baṣrī رحمه الله, we can feel the violation of our soul inside of us as soon as we sin. The Devil's plan was to make them eat from the tree, and he knew disobeying Allah ﷻ results in humiliation. This is Allah's ﷻ way of teaching Adam عليه السلام and Ḥawā', and through them, all of us, that, 'Some things I will make haram just like the tree, and the Devil will try to come in all directions to try to inch you closer to whatever I made haram, and will make you go there without you even realizing it, and then you will be humiliated'."[1]

Ibn al-Jawzī رحمه الله continued: "Do not get bored from standing [i.e. at the door of Allah's ﷻ Forgiveness and Mercy] even if you are reprimanded, and do not stop apologizing [for your sins] even if you are rejected. When a gate is opened for the incomers [i.e. those who attained Allah's ﷻ Love and Pleasure], rush to it fervently, lay down the head of humility and stretch out your hands while begging your Lord by saying,

be charitable unto us, [The Quran, 12:88]

so that the answer you may hear will be,

No blame will be upon you today... [The Quran, 12:92][2]

[1] Nouman Ali Khan.
[2] Ibn al-Jawzī, *Seeds of Admonishment and Reform*, pp. 114-116.

130

Ponder the mercy of Allah ﷻ and His way of dealing with the created. It is full of mercy even when He reprimands you! Ibn al-Qayyim رحمه الله writes, "There is [the hadith]: 'God is odd-numbered and loves the odd-numbered'. [Likewise,] He is compassionate and loves those who are compassionate, and is merciful to His compassionate servants. He also conceals [faults] and loves those who hide His servants' faults. He is clement and loves those who pardon; and is forgiving and loves those who forgive. He is gentle and loves those who are gentle to others. But He is angered by those who are coarse, rough and pompously callous.

He is companionable and loves brotherhood among men; forbearing and loves forbearance; good and loves virtuous deeds and those who perform them. He is just and loves justice. He accepts excuses and loves those who excuse His servants [for their errors]. And He recompenses His servant inasmuch as these attributes are present or absent in his soul!

So, He pardons whoever pardons, forgives whoever forgives, excuses whoever excuses, treats justly whoever treats justly. And God will befriend whoever befriends one of His servants. Whoever is merciful to creatures, to him is God merciful. Whoever does good for people, to him will God do good. Whoever is generous to them, to him will God be generous. Whoever benefits them, God will benefit him. Whoever conceals their faults, his faults God will conceal. And whoever excuses their errors, his errors God will excuse."[1]

---

[1] Ibn al-Qayyim, *The Invocation of God*, p. 41.

Allah ﷻ will never abandon us. When we do right by Allah ﷻ, Allah ﷻ will do right by us; and if I have gone away from Allah ﷻ, the only way for my life to get better is coming back to Allah ﷻ. Allah ﷻ says, "I will take care of you in the future but who has taken care of you all this time? I have been watching over you all this time."

This is a lesson for us. Remind yourself in desperate times that Allah ﷻ was there for you and remind yourself that Allah ﷻ is the same Master you have now. He is still there. You are not connecting to Him but that does not mean He is not connecting to you. The life of sin cannot sustain you; it is like an ocean whose water cannot be used because it is salty. Good deeds may look like dirt, but they are seeds that grow. If we want to have ease in this life, then Allah ﷻ will put us through some trial and only through that can we reach ease.

131

Allah ﷻ has subdued the earth as a mercy towards us. The default state of the earth is quakes and violent shaking. Therefore, what we are experiencing right now is an unnatural state of the earth. Allah ﷻ has subdued it until the Day comes when this mercy will be lifted and the earth will be allowed to erupt as it wants to.

> It is He who has made the earth manageable for you. [67:15]

You are a patch of dirt, yet you are not humble. If you are a patch of dirt that does not want to be humble, you want Allah ﷻ to let the earth act up like you do? Allah ﷻ subdued what we could never have subdued. Our provision on earth and the stability we enjoy, are all due to Allah ﷻ. And no matter how much you blossom in life, the ultimate blossoming will be when you return to Him. It is as though the default position is death and the only One holding death off from us is Allah ﷻ. The fact that you are alive is mercy. He is breaking your default position every day to keep you alive.

> What you have been given is only the fleeting enjoyment of this world. Far better and more lasting is what God will give … [The Quran, 42:36]

Nouman Ali Khan said, "It talks about all physical things and also life experience, in the sense what parents we have been given, what kind of youth, what friends, opportunity. All this is captured in that ayah. This ayah is making a commentary about my whole existence. The word use suggests that none of the things are actually mine. They are doors opened by Allah ﷻ. Allah ﷻ gave us all of the experiences and processes in our lives. Whether you remember them or are conscious of them or not. Allah ﷻ adds up all these to the enjoyment of the worldly life. So firstly, Allah ﷻ is saying that everything that happened, and all the experiences, happened partly because they will mature you. This is growth.

Everything in life is there to mature you. Secondly it means something that we benefitted from. Every experience, you can benefit from. There was good in it even if you could not see it. Also, people's views, either negative or positive, are worthless as well. People's comments on us change the way we see ourselves because we internalize those comments but then that is why the word of Allah ﷻ is there. It is there to make us see ourselves in the light of His words and not the words of people. To make us see who we truly are. So, we have two make two comparisons if we are going to survive: whatever Allah ﷻ has is better, and secondly, lasts longer. He gives in terms of *dunyā* and also in terms of the road to Jannah."

أَلَمْ يَأْنِ لِلَّذِينَ ءَامَنُوٓا أَن تَخْشَعَ قُلُوبُهُمْ لِذِكْرِ ٱللَّهِ

Has the time not yet come for believers' hearts to be humbled at the remembrance of Allah ... ?

This page intentionally left blank.

Journey 3

On the Matter of the Heart

The heart is the primary vehicle in which we journey towards Allah ﷻ. Rectifying the state of the heart rectifies all the rest of our affairs. Journeying back to Allah ﷻ requires the breaking of the various locks on our hearts in their various forms.

The Messenger of Allah ﷺ said: "Verily, there is a piece of flesh in the body, if it is healthy, the whole body is healthy, and if it is corrupt, the whole body is corrupt. Verily, it is the heart."[1]

So, we say:

يا مُقَلِّب القلوبِ ثَبِّت قَلبي على دِينِك

Yā muqallib al-qulūbi thabbit qalbī ʿalā dīnik

O Turner of Hearts, keep my heart steadfast on your *dīn* [religion]

---

[1] Al-Bukhārī and Muslim, *Riyāḍ al-Ṣāliḥīn*, no. 587.

This page intentionally left blank.

132

Dead Hearts and Empty Supplications

It is reported that Ibrāhīm b. Adham رحمه الله once passed through the market of al-Baṣrah. People gathered around him and asked: "O Abū Isḥāq, Allah the Exalted says in his Book, 'Call on me, I will answer your prayers,' but we have been calling on Him for a long time and He does not answer our prayers." [Ibrāhīm] replied, "O people of al-Baṣrah, your hearts have died in respect to ten things:

1. You know Allah but you do not give Him His rights;

2. You have read Allah's Book, but you do not act by it;

3. You claim to love Allah's Messenger ﷺ, yet you abandon his Sunnah;

4. You claim to be enemies to shaytan, but you conform to [his ways];

5. You say you love Paradise, yet you do not work for it;

6. You say you fear The Fire, yet you put yourselves closer to it [by sinning];

7. You say death is true, but you do not prepare for it;

8. You busy yourselves with the faults of others, and disregard your own;

9. You consume the favors of your Lord but are not grateful for them; and

10. You bury your dead but take no lesson from them."[1]

A wise man said: "A real man is the one who fears the death of his heart, not the death of his body. Most people fear the death of their bodies and are not concerned with the death of their hearts. They do not know of life except the material part of it."

"They found the right path, and hence walked on it,

> Indeed, those who have said, 'Our Lord is Allah' and then remained on a right course. [The Quran, 41:30]

When you exhale, giving out breaths of regret, they rise and form clouds, to patter upon you drops of forgiveness. And if you shed a tear on the cheek of repentance, you will give life to your barren heart."[2]

---

[1] Abū Nuʿaym, *Ḥilyat al-Awliyāʾ*, 8:15, 16.
[2] Ibn al-Jawzī, *Seeds of Admonishment and Reform*, pp. 151-152.

133

"Every sight, sound and thought that you allow to enter you, is like food for your heart. It can either enrich. Or it can poison. It all depends on the quality. You wouldn't drink poison. And you wouldn't eat mold. In the same way, don't allow poisonous and moldy food to enter your mind, eyes, or ears. Guard your heart, like you guard your body. Remember. even your body is temporary. Your heart and soul are not. They will move on from this fleeting life and will meet God in whatever condition you leave this world in. Keep them healthy.

What does that mean? It means that when you get a negative thought (demeaning self-talk, despair, doubt, fear), don't indulge it. Don't feed it or allow it to stay in the sanctuary of your mind and heart. When you come across immodesty or anything you shouldn't be looking at on the street or on the screen lower your gaze and protect your heart. When you hear indecency, guard your ears, and protect your heart."[1]

> The day when there will not benefit [anyone] wealth or children,
>
> but only one who comes to Allah with a sound heart. [The Quran, 26:88-89]

Ustadh Semir Nour said, "We must learn to monitor our thought process to remain calm and guided throughout our actions and stay peaceful. We often have a habit of thinking a certain way which our brain has got used to it, so we do not immediately realize the harm of this kind of thinking and that of jumping to certain emotions. We have to slow down this process. Whatever comes out of the mouth and

[1] Yasmin Mogahed.

257

in actions is a product of what is in the heart so one ought to trace it back to the heart to understand why that thing was said and what led it to being said or such action.

Monitoring thoughts allows you to trace the process back to the instigator and what led to you doing that action. The mind either trains itself to be strong or weak in being logical. The mind knows the ultimate consequences of following the desires and plunging the heart in destruction. Following the mind allows the mind to become confident in asserting itself (in being logical). However, ignoring the mind makes the mind weak and not confident in controlling you, therefore it gives up trying."

134

Allah ﷻ tells us,

> Do not follow blindly what you do not know to be true: ears, eyes, and heart, you will be questioned about all these. [The Quran, 17:36]

Therefore, whatever is taken in affects the heart one way or another. It will either bring you closer to Allah ﷻ or farther from Allah ﷻ. Constantly being on guard and rewatering our hearts is vital to constantly drawing close to Allah ﷻ.

"If the love you have for Allah ﷻ is more than anything else, then you are on your purpose. The root of all problems is loving something more than Allah ﷻ (whether that be a desire, an object, a person, etc.). Contemplating on Allah's ﷻ names and attributes, we start loving Allah ﷻ more because we understand who Allah ﷻ is and how He ﷻ constantly takes care of us and is concerned for us. In all decisions, we have to favor Allah ﷻ. We must increase the love for Allah ﷻ so much that then we are able to choose Allah ﷻ over anything else. In our journey to Allah ﷻ we have to have a healthy heart in heeding the warnings of Allah ﷻ.

The heart and deeds:

- The heart can tell you whether a path is the path of Allah ﷻ or not. You can detect whether your own self is tricking you or not. Allah ﷻ has instilled this in us. On the authority of Wābiṣah bin Ma'bad ؓ who said: I came to the Messenger of Allah ﷺ who said, "You have come to ask about righteousness." I said, "Yes." He ﷺ said, "Consult your heart. Righteousness is that about which the soul feels at ease and the heart feels tranquil. And wrongdoing is that which wavers in the soul and causes uneasiness in the breast, even though people have repeatedly given their legal opinion [in its favor]."[1]

- There are those will come and hijack your journey to Allah ﷻ and stop you and become a distraction for you. [The heart helps in] detecting when destructors appear on your path."[2]

The only solution is you being with Allah ﷻ, He is the only refuge. Three corrupters will be explored in the subsequent pages.

Ibn al-Qayyim رحمه الله says: "Doubtless, a heart grows tarnished like brass or silver, and its polish is by remembrance, which may make it shine like a crystal mirror. So, when one neglects remembrance it tarnishes, and when he returns it shines. Since the heart is tarnished by two things, heedlessness and sin, it is polished by two things; remembrance and asking for forgiveness. If heedlessness dominates most of someone's time, the tarnish on his heart grows in proportion. And if the heart is tarnished, it ceases to reflect things as they are. Therefore, it sees the false as true and the true as false. As the tarnish grows thicker, the heart grows dimmer, until it no longer reflects reality at all. And if this tarnish builds up, blackens, and envelops the heart completely, the heart's reflective quality and perception will be totally lost, so that it will neither accept what is true nor reject what is false. Such a fate is the worst that can befall it."[3]

---

[1] A ḥasan hadith transmitted from the *Musnads* of the two imams, Aḥmad ibn Ḥanbal and al-Dārimī, with a good chain of transmitters.
[2] Shaykh Semir Nour, Corrupters of the Heart (lecture), based on the work of Ibn al-Qayyim.
[3] Ibn al-Qayyim, *The Invocation of God*, p. 47.

As our beloved Messenger Muhammed ﷺ made the dua: "I seek refuge in the light of Your Face by which all darkness is dispelled and every affair of this world and the next is set right, lest Your anger or Your displeasure descends upon me. I desire Your pleasure and satisfaction until You are pleased. There is no power and no might except by You."

135

1. Excessive/unnecessary mingling with people

An analogy: if you are journeying from one city to another, your journey depends on whether your car is in good condition or not. Whether you can drive fast or not depends on the clarity of your vision because of weather, the state of your windshield, and so forth. The journey to the Hereafter depends on your heart. Every time you encounter humans, it is as though these people take a breath on your windscreen. You can see less, thus you have to slow down as a result. It is not only mist they blow onto your windscreen which at some point will cover it completely. The smoke and darkness resulting from the distance from Allah 🕮 will continue affecting your heart, making you stop completely at some points. For example, when someone criticized you and you keep thinking about what they said. All of this would have been avoided had you not excessively intermingled. They will burden your heart with something you cannot bear. You will be affected in worldly affairs too, not only the Hereafter. You will be too busy looking after them and split your mind on how you should be with this person and that and so forth. Was there any reason other than people who stopped Abū Ṭālib [the uncle of the Prophet 🕮] from believing on his deathbed?

This excessive intermingling is a result of expected benefits, affections, desires or loves, but when they are achieved, these fall apart and turn into animosities. Only that which is for Allah 🕮 lasts. What is the solution? To control these interactions and to intermingle with people in acts of obedience to Allah 🕮.

When you decide not to fit in, shaytan will come in convincing you that you cannot be right and all these people wrong, but rather you are just showing off. Do not look at shaytan when you are doing the right thing and trying to make the situation better. Make sure you fight these thoughts. Ibn al-Qayyim رَحِمَهُ ٱللَّٰه says: "These counsels and leaving such companies is not easy. It is easy for the one Allah makes it easy for." Make sure you do whatever you do with Allah ﷻ and while seeking His aid. All you need is to be truthful with Allah ﷻ.

136

2. Wishful thinking, following one's desires or hoping for unattainable things or visions

These can be based on something realistic but usually are thoughts in the mind that are unattainable—having irrational ideas. The person follows their desires in order to achieve something—but they are wishful thoughts, not practical things, such as, "Allah ﷻ will forgive me, I will go to Paradise regardless." Such a person may follow any desire, comforted by the wishful thinking that Allah ﷻ is the most merciful, therefore they open the door to being tricked by shaytan.

The corrupters of the heart make them lose sight of consequences or the willpower to go against their desires. The heart will be unable in such cases to distinguish between what is beneficial and what is not. They enjoy whatever they want and have wishful thoughts of everything coming out well in the end.

Someone who has intellect knows his actions will have consequences when they sin. Following desires will make them end up in the Fire. Not going against you desires will make you lose the willpower and determination to do anything good beyond the most basic things. Every time you set your mind to do something good, you find yourself unable to do it. They end up preferring only what is easy.

All people under the shade of Allah ﷻ have something in common: they refrain from their desires. Those who truly love Allah ﷻ are with Allah ﷻ in their thoughts and with their hearts. As ʿAlī bin Abī Ṭālib ؓ said: "They live in this world with their bodies, but their souls cling to Allah ﷻ."

An ancient poet said[1]:

You disobey Allah while you claim that you love Him
This is an offensive act
If your love had been true, you would have obeyed Him
A lover always obeys his beloved

Once you are in the ship of wishful thinking, it will be hard to find shore. Shaytan tells such people that Allah ﷻ will forgive them, so they do not need to worry. The strong waves of the ocean will throw such people from one desire to the next. While their opposites are those who always try to maximize their time and to be most productive and have a humble attitude of always seeking more knowledge and acting upon it—they are not laid back from wishful thinking.

Ibn al-Jawzī رَحِمَهُ اللهُ says to this effect, "Know that if the inner self knows that you are serious it will also be serious and hardworking, and if it knows that you are indolent it will become your master. From among the practices of discipline of the self is bringing it to account for every statement, for every action, for every negligence and sin. When its discipline is over, it will appreciate the exhaustion it endured."[2]

Ibn al-Jawzī رَحِمَهُ اللهُ continues, "Indeed, human beings are favored over beastly animals with the intellect that is designated to restrain one from following desires, therefore when a person does not accept the judgment of his intellect and abides by the judgment of his desires, the beastly becomes better than him. From the indicative signs through

---

[1] Taken from Ibn Rajab al-Ḥanbalī, *Jāmiʿ al-ʿUlūm wa-l-Ḥikam*, p. 539.
[2] Ibn al-Jawzī, *Disciplining the Soul*, p. 97.

which the excellence of contradicting [one's own] desires is proven is the honoring and the superiority of hunting dogs over other dogs, which is due to their ability to contradict their desires and to keep what they hunt for their master out of fear of punishment or as a show of appreciation.

Know that whims and desires call to attaining pleasure without taking into consideration its consequences, though one might know that this satisfaction will bring distress that actually exceeds it [i.e., exceeds the satisfaction]. Nonetheless whims and desires turn one away from reflecting on all this, which makes one lower to the exact state of animals. However, animals are excused because they do not observe the consequences of what they do. Be aware that [the intellect] is knowledgeable as well sincere in its advice, he should be patient upon what the intellect orders him to do, because knowing the excellence of the mind is enough for him to favor it. For has glory ever deteriorated, honor has been disgraced and humiliated or a bird hunted except as a result of following whims and desires?"[1]

A poet said regarding this,

How much satisfaction that provoked happiness,
Ended up revealing sadness and sorrows

How many desires ripped from their participants
The garment of religion and virtue

To overcome such wishful thinking and rescue yourself:

[1] Ibid, pp. 26-27.

- Determination: those who are enslaved [by their desires], they are enslaved for a long period and no longer have a sense of honor and do not feel determined and cannot think. So, develop within yourself determination that you are a free person. You are worthy of Paradise and must not engage in these behaviors.

- A dose of patience: remind yourself when you try to endure that your desirous self will give up soon after. Ibn al-Qayyim رَحِمَهُ اللهُ says it is only one hour. This bravery is required for one hour, for a short period, before your desirous self gives up. You and your desirous self are opponents looking at the strengths and weaknesses of each other.

- Thinking and imagining of what would happen if you overcame this desire: Think of yourself as already having done it and make it vivid.

- Internal mindsets: you need to think about knowledge. Just sitting, reading, and listening is not enough. You have to apply your mind. Remind yourself of the consequences of your sins. This will maintain your station with Allah ﷻ and the community of believers.

- You have to overcome your enemy and win the battle—determination will improve as a result of this. Your mind will start developing a successful track record and will be inclined to succeed.[1]

---

[1] See *Atomic Habits* by James Clear.

- Know that by committing this sin, you are in fact, telling Allah ﷻ, "No, I will not obey you," which if you truly ponder upon is a scary thought. It is as if you are challenging Allah to punish you.

137

3. Attachment to other than Allah ﷻ

Being attached to something makes it superior to you, because you perceive it as such. You do so by clinging to someone or something. You think you need it. You think all your success and happiness lies with this image or person. You become humbled and submissive to whatever you cling to. This creates the worst type of corruption for the heart. The highest state of heart is loving Allah ﷻ and disliking whatever distracts you from Him. This is 1) loving Allah ﷻ, 2) submitting to Allah ﷻ, 3) eagerly marching towards Him because all you want is Allah ﷻ, 4) turning away from anything other than Allah ﷻ. These people come back to Allah ﷻ no matter what. Understanding that everything and all the goodness of this world lies in the hands of Allah ﷻ will make you aim only at Allah ﷻ.

The heart was created for the worship of Allah ﷻ. Using it for anything else will make it corrupt. You will not achieve your ultimate purpose and will damage your most precious means of transportation. This can be the case for any devices Allah ﷻ gave us. This condition also corrupts the hearing, sight and understanding of the heart to perceive realities. Clinging to other than Allah ﷻ will destabilize the senses of the heart. The mention of Allah ﷻ to such locked hearts feels restricting to their pleasures, so they turn away. The heart by its very nature clings onto things, so your role is to not expose it to other than Allah ﷻ or what will distance you from Him. Do not let your eyes see and hear things other than what Allah ﷻ wants because if you do, your heart will cling to them.

The shaytan comes to you and entices you to do something entertaining but not forbidden [after you are tired from worship, etc.], but once you cling to that entertainment [other than Allah ﷻ], then thinking and doing haram from there is easy. The most forsaken and abandoned person is the one who attaches their heart to other than Allah ﷻ. That thing will abandon you and become a source of regret. And when it comes to people who say they are happy without being religious: 1) they have sadness inside of them that they do not want to admit, 2) or they are not conscious of their losses.

138

How is your heart? Do you make dua for your heart?

The Prophet ﷺ said, "The faith of a slave cannot be correct until his heart is correct,"[1] so ask Allah ﷻ:

- To guide your heart: "O Allah (ﷻ) guide my heart, correct my tongue and remove the spite of my heart."[2]

- To fill it with light: "O Allah (ﷻ) place light in my heart."[3]

- To make it firm: "O Turner of the hearts, make my heart firm on Your religion."[4]

- To cleanse it: "O Allah (ﷻ)! Wash my heart with the water of snow and hail, and cleanse my heart from all sins as a white garment is cleansed from filth."[5]

- To protect it: "Our Master, let not our hearts deviate after You have guided us and grant us from Yourself mercy. Indeed, You are the Bestower." [The Quran, 3:8]

- To make it sound: "I ask You for a sound heart and a truthful tongue."[6]

---

[1] *Musnad Aḥmad*, no. 13071.
[2] *Musnad Aḥmad*, no. 1997.
[3] *Ṣaḥīḥ al-Bukhārī*, no. 6316.
[4] *Al-Tirmidhī*, no. 3522.
[5] *Ṣaḥīḥ Bukhārī*, no. 6368.
[6] *Sunan an-Nasa'i*: 1304

- To cool it: "O Allah (ﷻ), cool my heart with snow, hail, and old water. O Allah (ﷻ), cleanse my heart of sins as You cleanse a white garment of filth."[1]

- To beautify it: "O Allah (ﷻ), make us love belief and adorn our hearts with it."[2]

"Not a leaf falls but He knows. Do you really think He is unaware of your heart? Seek comfort through patience and prayer. Indeed the Almighty's help is near."[3]

[1] *Al-Tirmidhī*, no. 3547.
[2] *Al-Adab Al-Mufrad*, no. 699.
[3] Maryam Khattak.

139

God is the Light of the heavens and earth. His Light is like this: there is a niche, and in it a lamp, the lamp inside a glass, a glass like a glittering star, fueled from a blessed olive tree from neither east nor west, whose oil almost gives light even when no fire touches it—light upon light—God guides whoever He will to his Light ... [The Quran, 24:35]

"Allah ﷻ calls Himself light. When Allah ﷻ lights something up, there is no comparison. Why do we need light? Life wouldn't exist without light. In the same way, if we don't have the light of guidance, we would be as good as dead. When you have the light of faith, you see beauty in everything. In the same way, you can't even see yourself without light in front of a mirror. We don't even know our own selves without knowing Allah ﷻ. Therefore, without light we don't know reality (you can't tell what's in front of you, what you should approach and what to avoid). Light is hope. The word 'surah' is used for what protects outside of a city and the passage of light in the center is protecting the heart just like the outside walls protect the city, the ribcage protects the heart.

You have an arch (your ribcage). Arched to give more light, allowing it to spread more. You have a lamp inside your ribcage (your heart) and you have to keep its glass clean so that the light can spread. The clean glass is a pure heart that is constantly cleaned from attacks of the Devil, of desires, of impulses and so forth. The oil inside is the soul Allah ﷻ gave you. When the light of guidance comes from Allah ﷻ, it lights up the light that Allah ﷻ already gave you [your heart]. So when you have light, you will be able to see clearly and the way you see the world changes. Inside of you there is something pure that will always come back to Allah ﷻ. No person is beyond hope; Allah ﷻ describes us with light inside of us.

"Its oil almost catches fire even without fire." Allah ﷻ says if you clean yourself and keep your glass clean, you'll automatically be inclined towards seeking something and it doesn't matter if you are Muslim or not. Light upon light: the light inside of you meets the light from the highest heavens (the Quran) then you can see. If you have light in your eyes but no light outside you can't see and if you have light outside but no light in your eyes, you still can't see; so if the Quran is there but your heart isn't clean, you still can't see even if you are listening to it and if you have a clean heart and haven't given Quran a chance then your vision is limited. Having the light of Allah ﷻ, everything becomes a reminder and sign for you, such as seeing a tree and understanding its roots are *lā ilāha illa 'llāh* and its branches are the good deeds that benefit everyone. As humans we run after things constantly. We have met Allah ﷻ when we were souls only and got directly exposed to His perfection, beauty and light. The light is still inside you because you were in His presence. You feel connected to the Quran because it is similar to what you experienced when you were in Allah's ﷻ presence."[1]

The Quran is advice from Allah ﷻ, and it does not come for free. If you love Allah ﷻ, your heart will propel you towards wanting to learn it. Understanding it with the mind is easy. It comes at the price of our hearts being engaged, in humility, in the desire to learn and the sincere promise to Allah ﷻ that we will do everything it takes to learn it.

> Is it not time for believers to humble their hearts to the remembrance of God and the Truth that has been revealed,

[1] Nouman Ali Khan.

and not to be...whose hearts hardened and many of whom were lawbreakers? Remember that God revives the earth after it dies ... [The Quran, 57:16-17]

O who you have believed, the moment you gained faith and found the light, you are reminded of this, when the *īmān* became conscious in your heart, as if Allah ﷻ is calling on us to go back to that moment and have that energy. "So many claim to be Muslim, you don't feel anything. Isn't it about time you feel something? What is the point of increasing knowledge when your heart has not moved as a result? The end is the heart. Their hearts should be filled with awe with the words of Allah ﷻ that came with the truth. Isn't it time they take their first steps towards that mission? Allah ﷻ answers the question you would have: how to fix it.

Allah ﷻ gives life to the dead land. The earth dies just like the heart dies. It doesn't matter how long the soil has been dry, water will make it grow but will take work and commitment. The revelation is the water bringing the dead heart back to life. Allah ﷻ has given you the water—you have to use it. The Quran is compared to water by Allah ﷻ. Our bodies need daily intake of water for survival and health. People that don't drink enough end up with chronic problems of all kinds. Hydration is key to well-being. The analogy necessitates that we feed our hearts daily with Allah's ﷻ words. They will help restore hope, help with grief, help control anger, fight evil temptations, control negative thoughts, and fill the heart with thoughts of gratitude and trust in Him and His counsel. Let's be healthy. Let's hydrate our hearts and souls every day."[1]

---

[1] Ibid.

140

Shaykh Semir Nour, may Allah ﷻ reward him, explained regarding the states of our hearts and their journey to Allah ﷻ, "The purpose of our existence is to get our souls the closest we can to our Creator. This is a spiritual journey that Allah ﷻ calls in the Quran *tazkiyah*. The aim of this journey is to improve our relationship with Allah ﷻ, until one gets to the point where nothing is more important or more pleasing to one's heart than being with Allah ﷻ and doing something that is pleasing to Him.

One of the most basic (yet most powerful) principles in the field of *tazkiyah*, is the following rule: Our hearts are like magnets, they're designed to develop interest, gravitate toward, and become passionate about anything they come in contact with—good or bad! Anything (absolutely anything) your heart comes in contact with, and becomes exposed to, your heart will develop interest in and gravitate toward it, become used to it, then become comfortable with it, and, ultimately, become in love with it—and even become addicted and dependent on it for a sense of peace and contentment. On the flip side of things, anything your heart in currently in love with, good or bad, if it stops coming in contact with it, it'll gradually become less and less interested in it, until it eventually forgets about it altogether—no matter how attached it was to it initially. Based on this principle, one can say the following: the key to loving anything you want to develop love toward, is to get your heart to become exposed to it, and to frequently and continuously come in contact with it. And the key to cleansing your heart from an attachment it may have to anything, is to reduce the times it comes in contact with it, and with time, it will certainly lose interest in it, and become used to being away from it.

This is an extremely powerful principle every Muslim must be aware of and be always mindful of. Think of how many acts of righteousness you can introduce in your life simply by following this principle. And think of how simple it can be to abandon addictive sins one may have always thought it impossible to quit. SubhanAllah! Did you ever wonder why Allah 🟦 wants you to make sure you have *khushūʿ* when you offer ṣalāh [i.e., make sure you connect your heart with the sayings and the movements of ṣalāh]? Have you ever wondered why shaytan does absolutely everything he can to prevent you from having *khushūʿ*? He actually works so hard to whisper, so aggressively, when one is performing ṣalāh. Did you ever wonder why?

Allah 🟦 wants your heart to come in contact and get exposure to the sweetness of standing before Him, knowing that you will eventually love it and become addicted to it—even if at the beginning you don't find that sweetness. For the same reason, shaytan will do everything he can to prevent that connection from taking place, because he knows, with enough instances of the heart connecting with ṣalāh, he could lose control over your heart, for good! With the same token, think of why Allah 🟦 instructs you to ponder and reflect, and to ensure that your heart is present when you recite the Quran? And ask yourself why shaytan puts so much effort in preventing you from reciting the Quran altogether or, failing that, he will make sure your heart does not connect with your recitation of the Quran?

Because of the above, our Gracious and Most Merciful Rabb, instructs us to be mindful of what we allow our hearts to come in contact with: 1) the sounds and voices we hear through our ears, 2) the visions and sights we see with our eyes, and 3) the thoughts that are thrown in our minds by our *nafs* [inner self or desiring self] or by shaytan. These are the channels of exposure! The heart connects with the outside world through these three channels. Your mission, in your journey is to make sure that nothing but good comes in contact with your heart through these three channels.

> Do not follow that which you have no knowledge of [i.e., you have no reliable knowledge that its beneficial or not harmful to your heart]: ears, eyes, and intellect, you will be questioned about all these. [The Quran, 17:36]

The good news is that Allah ﷻ created our hearts with the characteristic described above, but with His Grace and Mercy He also instilled in them *fiṭrah*, which is the natural disposition of the heart that makes it more inclined toward acts of righteousness and less inclined toward evil deeds [The Quran, 30:30]. This means that the time and effort needed to develop love toward righteous deeds are much less than the time and effort needed to develop love toward evil deeds—provided you ensure that your heart connects and feels the sweetness of every righteous deed you engage in. Imagine if one can engage with the righteous deeds, at least in the same level the heart connects with the pleasures of sins when committing them!"

Allah ﷻ says:

> Surely in this is a reminder for whoever has a mindful heart and lends an attentive ear. [The Quran, 50:37]

141

The more your heart receives wholesome nourishment [Islamic/spiritual knowledge], the stronger it gets and, hence, the more competent it becomes at restraining and controlling its desires. The great scholar of hadith Ibn Ḥibbān رَحَمَهُاللَّه, said: "A wise person must be more keen to strive and struggle to provide the highest quality nourishment for his heart, than he would for his physical body. For just as the physical body would become weak then die due to lack of food and drink, so will the heart—it will become weakened at first, and then eventually die in the absence of regular nourishment of knowledge and wisdom."[1]

Based on the above statement, compare the effort, time and money you put in feeding your physical body versus feeding your heart. What is the ratio? It is astonishing how much we wrong ourselves, is it not? Could this be the answer to why we struggle to restrain and control our desires? Could this be the answer to why we love Allah ﷻ but fail to worship Him as much as we would love to? Could it be the answer to why we want Paradise so badly but are so unable to do something meaningful to achieve it? Is our heart malnourished in some way? Is it even still alive? All that depends on how regular it receives its feeding. The quality of the nourishment your heart receives determines whether it will overpower your desires, or not.

> He grants wisdom to those whom He wills; and whoever is granted wisdom has indeed been granted abundant good. Yet

---

[1] *Rawḍat al-ʿUqalāʾ*.

none, except people of understanding, take heed. [The Quran, 2:269]

Ibn al-Jawzī رحمه الله said: "What a pity! If they were to truly know whom they had detached themselves from, they would prefer to be torn apart [instead]. Therefore, buy the salvation of your soul while the market is still open and its price is being offered and pay no heed to the whispers that entice you towards negligence and indifference, for indeed what may happen tomorrow can never be relied upon. How has the knock of exhortation been heard and yet none have listened to it; indeed this is meant

to warn whoever is alive ... [The Quran, 36: 70]"[1]

---

[1] Ibn al-Jawzī, *Seeds of Admonishment and Reform*, p. 100.

142

How to Contemplate the Quran by Sheikh Muhammad Bazmool

Whenever you read an ayah, first become acquainted with its meaning, and then ask yourself: What is it that Allah ﷻ wants to teach me with this ayah? Whenever you read an ayah that contains a story, contemplate what the lesson from this story is and what is its purpose. Whenever you read an ayah, look at its wording and ask yourself: why does this ayah use this wording instead of something else? Why is this expression used here, with this word order, rather than something else? So, grab hold of the rungs of the ladder to knowledge. Whenever you read a surah, think deeply about links and connections between the different subjects it contains, and what these different sections are driving towards.

You will find a wellspring of meanings and a mine of benefits, guidance, and clarity in the Quran, so don't lose out on this! Major scholars have expressed their regret at being preoccupied [away] from the Quran—even while some of them died with the Quran in their hands! So do not neglect the Quran, neither reciting it, nor understanding it, nor contemplating it, nor acting upon it! Take it as a guidance and a way of life!

Whenever you hear an ayah with a call [i.e., "O' you who believe..."], then listen to it, for it either contains some good which you are commanded to do or some evil which you are prohibited against. Know with complete certainty that nothing has been placed in the Quran without a reason. Every single letter has a meaning, and every arrangement of words indicates something. No word has been substituted for another except that it holds a message, and no word has been included or omitted except that it signals something. So, engage with the Quran with this type of attitude; it will open the doors to understanding for your mind.

Some assume that the Quran is really hard or that its meanings are locked away. Allah ﷻ says it's not the Quran that has locks but rather the hearts that don't give it the effort or time for contemplation. That means the hearts have other things locking them up; other things preoccupying them, other things making them curious, other things seemingly more worthy of contemplation. I must ask myself a difficult but honest question.

In the moments when my mind is free during my waking day, what is my heart locked up thinking about? This book will bring protection, joy, counsel, healing, relief, blessings that will stay with you and me ... all of that if your hearts unlock a bit from all the other stuff and give themselves to it. What have my heart's other preoccupations brought me?

143

The basis of Allah's ﷻ love and mercy is rectifying the state of our hearts, because He knows that is our salvation and success in this world and the next. Ibn al-Qayyim رَحِمَهُ اللهُ said, "The heart, in its journey to Allah, Majestic is He, is like that of a bird: love is its head, and fear and hope are its two wings. When the head and two wings are sound, the bird flies gracefully. If the head is severed, the bird dies ... if the bird loses one of its wings, it then becomes a target for every hunter or predator."[1]

"People have the mindset where the religion has something to offer for you, the entire promise is that something will get better in this life. The Quran paints a different picture: things get worse after turning to Islam. The Quran gives a harsh reality check: exhausting labor is what this life is. This life isn't luxury nor suffering. A good life in the Quran means that no matter what storms happen and what people do, there is calm inside you, you are content with Allah ﷻ, and you know whatever you are going through is going to come and go, and the only real treasure you need to protect is your faith.

Other things will come and go and that doesn't matter. Even when smacked by the storm, this is a course of action that is guiding me even though it may not be part of what I planned. One step being closer to Allah ﷻ is the goal itself. That is what is to be inspired for. The small steps are the goal themselves. He put me here to guide me.

Impurities cannot come out unless we are put under extreme test. Allah ﷻ will expose those who are honest and who are liars. Allah ﷻ

---

[1] *Madārij al-Sālikīn*, 1/390.

is saying to those tested, it is not your problem how and when I give these evildoers justice, on My terms. Whoever hopes they will meet with Allah ﷻ, that meeting is coming, meaning if you never lost hope in Allah ﷻ no matter what happened knowing Allah ﷻ knows all that happened to you. Whoever continues to do the right things, they are doing it for themselves. You are not doing Allah ﷻ a favor.

Allah ﷻ doesn't need any of us. Allah ﷻ is saying if you don't let go of your faith, He will reward us with the very best we did. Then Allah ﷻ speaks about the parents: parents are the biggest trial. You will have to make a choice between you listening and trusting Allah ﷻ that He will guide your heart, or you will go with your own self and trust yourself more than Allah ﷻ and His messenger ﷺ. When you obey Allah ﷻ, He will be the one to see you through your problems and the only one able to help you. What Allah ﷻ gives you is the solution. Obeying Allah ﷻ will get me out of my problem."[1]

[1] Nouman Ali Khan.

144

"Hide your good deeds the way you hide your bad deeds. Do not be amazed by your actions, for you do not know whether you will be [amongst those who will be] happy or wretched [on the Day of Judgment]."[1]

Shaykh al-Islam Ibn Taymiyyah رحمه الله said, "The one who is sincere towards Allah ﷻ has tasted the sweetness of true servitude toward Him, which keeps him from becoming enslaved by anything else, and he has tasted the sweetness of loving Allah ﷻ, which keeps him from loving anything else. For the sound heart, there is nothing sweeter or more delightful than the sweetness of faith, which includes servitude to, love for and sincerity towards Allah ﷻ. This means that the heart is attracted towards Allah ﷻ, turning to Him, fearing Him, and putting its hope in Him.

The one who loves will fear losing the thing he is seeking, or getting the thing he dreads, so the slave of Allah ﷻ who loves Him must always be between hope and fear. If the slave is sincere towards Allah ﷻ, He will choose him, revive his heart, and bring him close to Him, and will turn away from him all evil and shameful deeds that contradict that. He fears attaining the opposite of that, unlike the heart that is not sincere towards Allah ﷻ, which has a will and is seeking for something to love, although this love is not focused and may fall in love with anything he comes across and happens desire. The heart is like the branch of a tree which may be swayed and bent by any passing breeze, so sometimes the heart may be attracted to images, forbidden or otherwise, and so it remains a prisoner, enslaved by

---

[1] Imam al-Bayhaqī, *Shuʿab al-Īmān*, no. 6412.

something which, if it had become a slave to him, it would have been something to be ashamed of.

If a person is not sincere towards Allah 薬 and does not become His slave, so that his heart is enslaved by his Lord alone, with no partner or associate, and Allah 薬 is dearer to him than all else, and he is humble and submissive towards Him, he will be enslaved by created beings and the devils will dominate his heart, so he will be one of the misguided brothers of the devils and will be overwhelmed by evil and shameful deeds, the extent of which Allah 薬 alone knows. This is the way it is, there can be no other way."[1]

[1] Ibn Taymiyyah, *Al-'Ubūdiyyah*.

145

I remind you to protect your heart before it is too late with to regard to Allah ﷻ. Following desires and sinning is detrimental to the state of the heart and gives the Devil considerable power over you. Wake up before you are woken up [resurrected] once and for all on the Day of Decision, when nothing will benefit you, neither your regret, nor your wealth. Ibn al-Jawzī رحمه الله said, "This worldly life is a market where the clamor and tumult of desires fills the ears, therefore if you busy yourself with it, how would you be able to hear exhortation and beneficial preaching? The ant-prince of providential help calls out to the righteous to save themselves as the tribulation of Sulaymān السلام approaches: desist your base nature from consuming those morsels of worldly delights that you so desire[1]

> lest Sulaymān and his armies crush you, unperceiving. [The Quran, 27: 18]

Indeed, it is difficult to swim in a lake infested by crocodiles, to travel through a land populated by beasts. O you who are chained in the backyard of this mortal existence, censure is looming over you, yet you are unable to hear the counsel of sincere advice, as the glue in your ear prevents you! Woe to you, precious little time is left for you, so rush to benefit from what remains from the wick of the lamp [of your lifespan]; are you not even affected by the voice of exhortation? Do you not even feel pain from the lashes of sermon?

---

[1] The metaphor is that of the ants which were in the valley that Sulaymān and his soldiers were crossing. Had the ants not heeded the warning of their fellow ant to rush for safety, they would have been crushed by Sulaymān's army ﷺ.

O you who is settled in on his desires though he is but transient in this world; O you who wastes their capital of lifespan; when will you return to your senses? O you whose heart is blind to the degree that even [Prophet] 'Īsā [Jesus] ﷺ would not be able to heal it; O you whose idleness is even longer than the epoch of the cave dwellers' sleep; let us for the sake of argument, assume that death does not come all of a sudden! Do you not know what ailment might come all of a sudden?"[1]

He ﷺ continues in his attempt to awaken the reader from a sleep that is heavier than the sleep of the Companions of the Cave, "For this Allah ﷻ, Exalted is He, Commanded this worldly life to serve those who serve Him, and to enslave those who serve it. The pious does not pay attention to his shadow, therefore the shadow always follows him, while the one seeking it diligently all the time keeps looking around for it and is thus unable to see it. O the one devoted to this worldly life, for how long will you be lost in the desert of confusion? Does your persistent effort [in seeking the worldly life] have any limit? Will your hope [to remain in this life] ever end? Woe to you: the ocean never drains out, so be content with your share of the water. Woe to you: walking leisurely making small steps will never get you to your final destination! It is impossible for a person to feel sufficiency when he is not content with what he already has in his hand! Woe to you, all that you rejoice for in this life is actually what you should be sad for, if only you would realize.

Your excessive keenness is like a cloud that can block the bright sun of your intellect. This cloud prevents the heart from perceiving the Hereafter, therefore you should send the platoon of your strong will,

---

[1] Ibn al-Jawzī, *Seeds of Admonishment and Reform*, pp. 109-111.

to tear apart this hazy cloud into bits. You have what suffices you, nevertheless you seek what would ruin you.

This life is like wine; whenever the assiduous drinks from it, his thirst increases. It is sufficient for you to cover your parts with the garment of contentedness, for it casts away the concerns from your heart and replaces them with comfort. The example of a person attached to this life is like a bee that comes across a water lily, gets attracted by its scent and decides to settle upon its leaves. However, when night falls, the leaves draw back and get submerged in the water, and thus the bee meets its death. Do you not know that continuing to drink water even after your thirst has been extinguished will make you perpetually thirsty? How chained you are to this life! You have thrown yourself into the deep well of worldly love! When will piety arrive to rescue you from your condition, so that you would be among those who would hear the chants of joy:

... glad tidings ... [The Quran, 12:19]?"[1]

---

[1] Ibn al-Jawzī, *Seeds of Admonishment and Reform*, pp. 146-147.

146

Our hearts are the primary vessels carrying our light of faith; therefore the heart is the primary target of the Devil. A heart devoid of such light would be left alone by the Devil because such person is already doomed. Ibn al-Qayyim رَحِمَهُ اللهُ writes, "The hearts are likened to three chambers, the chamber of the king, which contains his treasures, supplies and jewels; the chamber of the servant, which contains his treasures and supplies, but none of the jewels or supplies of the king; and a chamber which is completely empty. If a thief came to rob any of these three chambers, which one would he choose? If you said the empty room, it would be absurd, for what is there to take? But it would be equally absurd if you think that he will rob the chamber of the king, there being so many guards around it that a thief cannot even get near. How could he, when the king himself is guarding it? How could he be approaching with all the guards and soldiers surrounding it? Therefore, nothing is left for the thief to rob except the other room, and that is the one he attacks.

Let the wise man ponder this analogy, and let it sink into his heart, for this is the way of the three hearts. The heart of the nonbeliever or the hypocrite, a heart devoid of all good, is the Devil's home. The Devil marks it for himself, claims it as his territory, takes residence and dwells in it. What is there for him to steal, when it already contains his stock and supplies, his doubts, deceits and whisperings? And what devil [dare approach] a heart filled with the majesty of God Almighty, with reverence, love, vigilance and modesty? If he would steal something from it, what would it be? His only hope is to snatch something surreptitiously from the servant. And that time is inevitable, the servant is but a human being, subject to laws which govern men; he will brook neglect, forgetfulness, confusion and compulsion. It is related that Wahb ibn Munabbih affirmed that in one of the sacred books [God says], 'I do not dwell in rooms which are not vast enough for Me, and what thing could be vast enough for Me, when my Footstool contains [all] the heavens? But I am in the heart of the one who has bid farewell to and left behind all else but Me.' This has the same meaning as the saying, 'My heavens and My earth do not contain Me, but the heart of My believing servant contains Me."[1] Ibn 'Abbās ﷺ said: "The Devil is perched upon the human heart. When a man forgets and grows heedless, the Devil begins to whisper, but when he remembers God Most High, the Devil flees."

---

[1] Ibn al-Qayyim, *The Invocation of God*, pp. 31-32.

147

Ibn al-Qayyim رحمه الله says: "The caller who calls to faith could be heard by any ear that listens, but Quranic exhortations have no meaning for hearts which are empty because doubtful things and passions have overwhelmed them. [For these hearts] the lamps have gone out, and heedlessness and ignorance are in control. [For them] the doors to guidance are locked shut, and even the keys have been lost. The rust of 'What they have earned' [The Quran 39:51 and others] has encrusted them. Drunk with the passion for sin and delusion, they are unreceptive to blame. Despite admonishments sharper than spears and arrows, they perish in an ocean of ignorance, heedlessness, deeply ingrained passions and desires. And 'for the wounds of the dead, treatment is of no avail'."[1]

Nouman Ali Khan said, "Everything is meaningful in that it leads to a larger purpose. We are not randomly flowing. It is all something incredible and valuable. Everything around us contains a sign pointing to Allah ﷻ. It has a sign in it. You have to dig in it, not the thing itself. You could look at the same mountains and sea but not everyone can see how this is pointing at the oneness of Allah ﷻ. There are miraculous signs for people that get to the point; they don't get distracted by side elements. They have a clear picture of who at heart they are. For example, they look at the code rather than the interface we see. When you don't see these signs, you put value on things that aren't actually valuable; then fake values assigned to us become valuable. These people understand value doesn't come from these things so they are unaffected by them. So, when these come and go,

---

[1] Ibn al-Qayyim, *The Invocation of God*, p. 68.

they don't feel less or more valuable. They see the true value of everything. They see the lesson in everything.

They got to pick up on this call and feel special for being chosen to pick up this call by Allah ﷻ. This call is open to all of creation, to all those willing to listen. Anybody who is willing to see and listen. The truth deserves to be shared because it is the truth—you become an extension of the call because you were called. We are slaves of Allah ﷻ. You're always a slave, it is your identity. By extension, your choice and lifestyle are defined by your Master. When Allah ﷻ calls us His slaves it means 'You are slaves to no one except Me'. It frees you from the superiority of other humans. It makes all humans equal. It also frees you from becoming a slave to yourself—a slave of fashion, people's opinion, culture, influences, peer pressure, or fear; this is the most powerful expression of freedom."

148

We simply cannot do without the protection of Allah ﷻ. Here we explore what it means to be protected by Sūrat al-Falaq [surah 113] and Sūrat al-Nās [surah 114]. Evil from outside is combatted by Sūrat al-Falaq, while evil from within [that starts building up because of the whisperings of the Devil or other humans] is combatted by Sūrat al-Nās. Allah ﷻ is mentioned once in Sūrat al-Falaq but three times in Sūrat al-Nās due the more dangerous state of the evil that comes from within—three times more desperate. Allah ﷻ is the one we turn because He fulfills every need. You cannot turn to anyone like you turn to Allah ﷻ. Allah ﷻ is saying your greatest need is to be protected and because He is al-Ṣamad [the One who fulfills all needs] then we need to turn to Him for protection on the inside and out.

Whatever Allah ﷻ made is for your benefit. But people use these things in a wrong way and these created things have the potential to be misused. The first thing we seek is acknowledging the tendency we have to misuse the things around us so O Allah ﷻ protect me from misusing them for evil and keep me from using anything you created for the wrong purpose and keep me from harm [as misuse leads to harm]. Allah ﷻ highlights three things He created: the night, evil of the ones blowing into knots, and the one who is jealous. But in al-Nās, we have three names of Allah ﷻ, but one evil that is mentioned. Allah ﷻ is saying we often do not want to share our feelings due to self-esteem and not wanting to be vulnerable. Allah ﷻ is saying when it comes to Me, do not let your self-respect or pride get in the way, and openly say I need protection. It is the necessary prerequisite for Allah's ﷻ protection. Allah ﷻ will not protect the one who does not come to Him with humility. We have to acknowledge the danger and humble ourselves. When we seek someone's protection, we honor them out of gratitude. So, we must be grateful and honor Allah ﷻ. When we come before Allah ﷻ for protection, we say O Allah [ﷻ] I'm done, I come to You for protection, please protect me. *Falaq* is something that tears open, or hard rock that cracks open. When a mountain breaks apart, it is also called *falaq*. It is also used for soft things such as tearing bread open, or for hard things such as cracking a pistachio nut open. The overall meaning is taking something that was originally hard and did not appear to have any breaks, getting to the depth of it, and tearing it open. He is the one who tears open every day for a new day. You are saying in effect in Sūrat al-Falaq that whatever dangers there are that seem unbreakable, I'm coming to the One who can break it and rip it open. We need Allah ﷻ to break night and darkness.

Ghāsiq [in verse 3 of the surah] refers to darkness; *ghasaqa* describes when a tear drips out, when a mother begins to give milk, when an injury has taken place and blood starts to flow, or when something bad has been unleashed from within and cannot stay contained. When the night experiences this, it is overwhelmed by darkness. Allah ﷻ is light and all else is darkness. We talk about both spiritual and physical darkness—Allah ﷻ brings you back from spiritual darkness into the light even if you are in the middle of darkness. I seek refuge with Allah ﷻ even when that little bit of light is gone, when I see no hope anywhere. When circumstances that are bad get worse, that is when you should remember that it is Allah ﷻ who can clear this. Allah ﷻ can tear darkness apart when no one else can. The Quran is healing for what lies inside the heart. Internalize Sūrat al-Falaq and you will be protected. You are outside and it's raining, and this is the building (Sūrat al-Falaq) you will find shelter in if you truly enter it wholeheartedly. This will protect you from any evil.

149

In Sūrat al-Falaq Allah ﷻ protects us from the problems of this world; while what is in the heart is what Sūrat al-Nās protects. It protects you from the dangers against your *dīn*. Allah ﷻ gave us one of His names to protect our world but three of His names to protect our faith since faith beautifies this world and the next. These three names do not occur together like this anywhere else. These names of Allah ﷻ refer to His divinity. Allah ﷻ has many names, but these three names in particular put us in awe of Him, for they capture our powerlessness and insignificance before Him. At the heart of worship are these three names.

Rabb [owner, master]: also used for ownership of small things. Usually when you have a dispute involving property, you go to the owner, then the ruler, then Allah ﷻ. Allah ﷻ here is saying by the usage of His three names that Allah ﷻ for you is all three. In our case it is Allah ﷻ from the smallest need to the greatest need. From the most immediate to the loftiest, you always turn to Him. *Rabb* is also associated with *rubb*, when you heat a drink to cleanse it of impurities so that only half of it is left.

It is also used for juice made of dates and heated until the thickest elements are left; or when a thick syrup is made from grapes. *Rubb* is used when you take something that was soft, and you harden it or toughen it to something else to make it mature so that you can put it to work. The relationship with Allah ﷻ is that He removes impurities and makes us strong and makes us of benefit. It also includes the process of getting there, in that Allah ﷻ takes you through it step by step. In Arabic usage, *rabb* is used to mean a giver of gifts, one in authority, an owner, or one who nurtures and maintains someone.

Rabb is someone in charge of you who takes care of you and makes sure you reach ultimate maturity. Thus, if I have a *rabb*, my needs are taken care of, I am protected, and he gifts me more than I need.

When the needs of the servants are taken care of, boundaries have to be set, and in order to set boundaries you need an authority. What greater authority than a king! Hence the logical progression of Allah's ﷻ names. Humans however always want to do more, to find something greater than themselves, and they never find satisfaction for this desire in anything in this worldly life. We constantly seek what is better and better, seeking perfection. This goal of this search in life is *ilāh* [deity]. Every creature can have a *rabb* [owner] and *malik* [king], but humans need an *ilāh* to worship. An *ilāh* is an object of love, longing, obsession, etc. When we seek Allah's protection ﷻ, we are saying this is the basis of my relationship with you O Allah ﷻ. I'm seeking your protection to keep the integrity of this relationship because something on the outside is influencing me and I'm losing my hold on this relationship, I'm losing my purpose.

First, you lose purpose [*ilāh*] and when your purpose becomes less than Allah ﷻ, you start crossing boundaries set [by *malik*—king], and when you do that, you start believing something or someone else will take care of you [instead of your true *rabb*]. You stop relying on Allah ﷻ. This happens when your highest goal is not Allah ﷻ. When whispers become prevalent, purpose goes away, boundaries disappear, and one does everything they want.

These people lose desire to live because they feel no one cares about them, they have no *rabb*. More about this progression of names is that in this profound order, Allah ﷻ is making us aware of the degrees of getting to know their Maker. By observing that one has blessings both on the inside and outside, they recognize they have someone taking care of them [a *rabb*]. Next, they then realize that the one taking care of them Himself has no needs and is above all that they can imagine [a *malik*]. Next you recognize if He is that high, then nothing should ever be a greater goal or obsession than Him [*ilāh*].

The repetition of "people" [*nās*] three times implies that you should hear this and know it is about yourself. As if to say 'O Allah (ﷻ) I am among the people and I have needs like the people', You are the caretaker, and nobody understands my problem like You do because You are the caretaker of everyone.' Moreover, your problem is coming from people, so it can be solved by the One who has the authority over them.

Sharr [in 114:4] is painful harm and also means evil. *Waswās* [in the same verse] is the clinking of jewelry which is barely heard. It is also used for a hunter perched, waiting to catch his prey and his dog is about to leap at the animal, and he tells the dog to wait, barely heard; also, a whisper that can barely be heard and is not intelligible. The implication is that it is a partial, not coherent, speech. "Did I just hear that, was that a word, or was it just noise?".

It also refers to subconscious suggestions that influence over you, discreet, subtle, barely detectable messages that you do not even realize are messages. The word suggests that the one who does it is very good at it. And if that is not enough, Allah ﷻ adds the words *khannās* after it, which is a star that you see, but which then disappears. Because of this you doubt that it was even there in the first place. It is also a barely noticeable gesture done by rabbits where they raise their nose.

There are two meanings, the first being to disappear without notice and the second, to delay somebody or slow them down so that they do not do what they were meant to do. These are whispers that delay you from what you were supposed to do and encourage you to keep putting it off for later, until you never do it. They put themselves in fitnah, for example, "Yes, I know what you are saying, parties are bad places, but I know how to handle myself—I can deal with it." You kept putting yourself in tribulation and in that environment and as a result you started putting off your mandate to change—you kept procrastinating, became doubtful, and your false wishes deluded you.

Allah ﷻ is saying there are dangers we do not recognize, and He is teaching us to say this even though we do not recognize them. There are dangers in these kinds of environments and in people that you do not recognize but He is telling you that you have to recognize, and they are very powerful. Words are very powerful, Allah ﷻ guides us with words. *Waswās* is someone who makes a sound, while *khannās* is a suggestion, therefore it can be body language, facial expressions, etc.

Every human has been assigned an associate devil who is constantly making suggestions. Shaytan is always there to make you do the worst possible thing. Someone says salam and the Devil makes you think this person is not sincere and actually dislikes you; or you see something bad and he will say it is not that bad, you did umrah a month ago, and you have so many good deeds, and Allah ﷻ is forgiving, and Ramadan is soon, etc. He disappears before you know it is him. Our chest is protected yet shaytan can get into the chest. But he cannot get into the heart. Only you can let him in. The thoughts in your head are not only you.

The surah climaxes with a final repetition of the word *al-nās*. As if to say that shaytan will do whispers but even more dangerous than that are people. These people have let shaytan in their hearts and they are as if ambassadors of shaytan. They make suggestions to you.

The connection with the previous surah: Allah ﷻ ended Sūrat al-Falaq with something that happens in the heart: *ḥasad* [envy]. *Ḥasad* is in the heart. Iblīs has more *ḥasad* and spite than anyone else. And now he is hovering around your heart waiting to get it, so here you are asking Allah ﷻ for protection and saying, "O Allah (ﷻ) if You let him in my heart, I will become jealous, spiteful, angry and desirous of seeing others go down."

Printed in Great Britain
by Amazon

42404262R00172